SCIENCE FICTION
as Literature

Science Fiction

AS LITERATURE

by John Aquino

nea

National Education Association
Washington, D.C.

Library of Congress Cataloging in Publication Data

Aquino, John.
    Science fiction as literature.

    (Developments in classroom instruction)
    Bibliography: p.
    1. Science fiction—Study and teaching. I. Title.
II. Series.
PN3448.S45A7   809.3'876   76-10715
ISBN 0-8106-1804-4

Acknowledgments

The manuscript has been reviewed by Helen M. Edmonston, retired teacher, Montgomery County (Maryland) Public Schools.

   The publisher gratefully acknowledges permission to quote from the following:

From "The Queen of Air and Darkness" by Poul Anderson. Copyright by Poul Anderson. Reprinted by permission of the author and the author's agents, Scott Meredith Literary Agency Inc., 845 Third Ave., New York, New York 10022.

Copyright 1970 by Ray Bradbury (THE MARTIAN CHRONICLES) reprinted by permission of Harold Matson Co. Inc.

Copyright 1951 by Ray Bradbury (THE ILLUSTRATED MAN) reprinted by permission of Harold Matson Co. Inc.

From "Arena" by Frederick Brown. Reprinted by permission of the author's literary agents, Scott Meredith Literary Agency Inc., 845 Third Ave., New York, New York 10022

Acknowledgments are continued on page 64.

CONTENTS

PASSWORTHY: If they don't come back—my son and your daughter—what of that, Cabal?

CABAL: Then, presently, others will go.

PASSWORTHY: Oh, God, is there never to be any age of happiness? Is there never to be any rest?

CABAL: Rest enough for the individual man—too much, and too soon, and we call it Death. But for Man no rest and no ending . . . . First this little planet with its winds and ways, and then all the laws of mind and matter that restrain him. Then the planets about him, and at last across immensity to the stars. And when he has conquered all the deeps of space and all the mysteries of time, still he will be beginning.

PASSWORTHY: But . . . we're such little creatures. Poor humanity's so fragile, so weak. Little . . . Little animals.

CABAL: Little animals. If we're not more than animals we must snatch each little scrap of happiness and live and suffer and pass, mattering no more than all the other animals do or have done. Is it this—or that: all the universe or nothing? Which shall it be, Passworthy? Which shall it be?

—H. G. Wells, *Things to Come*

1. What Is Science Fiction?

In his introduction to the anthology *One Hundred Years of Science Fiction*, Damon Knight, echoing Basil Davenport and C. S. Lewis, states that the practitioners of science fiction have never been able to agree on a definition.[1] Indeed, a problem in defining science fiction is that it has not been recognized as a valid literary genre. The term "science fiction" itself was not coined until 1929. Retroactively, examples of science fiction have been traced as far back as the writings of the Roman author Lucian in the second century A.D. But until the middle of this century, writers seemed to stumble into the specific genre by accident. Writers such as Poe, Bierce, Lovecraft, even the young Ray Bradbury, moved from fantasy to science fiction to straight fiction, depending upon which elements they wished to emphasize in a story.

Several definitions of science fiction have been proposed. Three are quoted below. All of them are relatively broad so as to include the many excursions that have been made into the scientific unknown since Lucian.

According to Kingsley Amis,

> Science fiction is that class of prose narrative treating of a situation that could not arise in the world we know, but which is hypothesized on the basis of some innovation in science or technology, or pseudo-science or pseudo-technology, whether human or extra-terrestrial in origin.[2]

According to Sam Moskowitz,

> Science fiction is a branch of fantasy identifiable by the fact that it eases the willing suspension of disbelief of its reader by utilizing atmosphere of scientific credibility for its imaginative speculations in physical science, space, time, social science, and philosophy.[3]

According to Donald A. Wollheim,

> Science fiction is that branch of fantasy, which, while not true of present day knowledge, is rendered plausible by the reader's recognition of the scientific possibilities of it being possible at some future date or at some uncertain period of the past.[4]

All of these definitions are acceptable. They cover science fiction possibilities ranging from space travel (*Rendezvous with Rama, The Martian Chronicles, From the Earth to the Moon, The First Men in the Moon*) to invasions of the earth (*Childhood's End, The War of the Worlds, Lord of Light,* "Farewell to the Master") to strange scientific inventions or discoveries (*The Invisible Man, Frankenstein, The Strange Case of Dr. Jekyll and Mr. Hyde, Twenty Thousand Leagues Under the Sea*) to portraits of the future (*Brave New World, I Am a Legend, Planet of the Apes,* "Flowers for Algernon," *1984*) to strange lands and other scientifically based adventures (*Lost Horizon, Fantastic Voyage*) to explorations of scientific concepts such as time—the fourth dimension—and other dimensions (*The Time Machine, Flatlands*). Although the definitions have some differences, the important aspects of all three are that science fiction is a) a prose narrative, b) concerns situations that could not occur in our time, and c) has a scientific credibility that enables the reader to suspend disbelief in these events that are not possible in everyday life.

But what is science fiction from the point of view of literary classification? Amis refers to it as a "class of prose narrative"—in other words, a genre under the form, fiction; Moskowitz and Wollheim state that it is a "branch of fantasy." Literary genres are

10

classified by "the nature, not the structure, of the meaning of the work, the genre of which is determined by the kind of object referred to (shepherds in a pastoral, heroes in epic, the marvelous in romance). . . ."[5] The objects described in science fiction are unknown worlds within a scientific reference. By utilizing our definitions of science fiction and of literary genres, science fiction, then, would be classed as a literary genre, or at least a sub-genre under fantasy.[6]

Science Fiction and Fantasy

What is the difference between science fiction and fantasy? Science fiction, in the definitions quoted above, is often seen as a branch of fantasy. "Fantasy," in this sense, is the prose narrative that concerns the creation of other worlds. There has developed, however, another sub-genre under the broad genre, fantasy; this sub-genre is called "pure fantasy." The difference between science fiction and pure fantasy is important for an understanding of science fiction.

Pure fantasy has been defined as "a narrative of marvels . . . The essence of this sort of story can be summed up in one word: magic."[7] Professor Tolkien, in his famous essay, "On Fairy Stories," goes so far as to define fantasy as complete sub-creation of another world.[8] Tolkien's definition excludes stories that end as dreams, such as *Alice in Wonderland*, and some critics have objected to this. At any rate, books that are often classed as pure fantasy include Tolkien's *The Hobbit* and the *Lord of the Rings*, T. H. White's *The Once and Future King*, W. H. Morris' *The Well at the End of the World*, James Stephens' *The Crock Of Gold*, Peter Beagle's *The Last Unicorn*, and several novels by Lord Dunsany including *The King of Elfland's Daughter*.

Pure fantasy and science fiction have many similar characteristics derived from fairy tales: the entry into another world; a journey; the gathering together of a band of experts. Characteristics of one are sometimes found in the other. Vampires appear in Richard Matheson's science fiction novel, *I Am a Legend*. (The twist is that they are creatures that plague the last man on earth.) And the concept of other dimensions (such as time, the fourth dimension), a science fiction staple, can be found in some fantasies: the Irish faerie land of the Shi, described by James Stephens in *The Crock of Gold* and *Irish Faerie Tales*, is another dimension into which unwary travelers sometimes wander.

11

Kingsley Amis notes that it could be hypothesized that an author could change a pure fantasy into a science fiction story by inserting scientific terms and explanations.[9] But this hypothetical case, rather than showing greater similarity between science fiction and pure fantasy, underlines their basic difference, which is one of emphasis. We have noted that the credibility of science fiction rests in scientific explanations and atmosphere. The credibility of pure fantasy is achieved by the actual creation of the other world, such as Tolkien's Middle Earth. Science fiction is a world that lies in scientific speculation. Fantasy is a world of magic, faeries, hobbits, and ghosts. In execution, then, although both contain other worlds, science fiction, with its emphasis on scientific and technological principles, is definitely based in our world. It allows for comments on our social functions and institutions, our religions, and our philosophies, comments that most pure fantasies lack.

It should be remembered that many landmark works of a "fantastic" nature seem to overlap the definitions of both pure fantasy and science fiction. For example, in C.S. Lewis' *Out of the Silent Planet* (1941), the entry into the other world is made by means of a rocket ship and the other world is Mars or, as it is called in the book, Malacandra. This would seem to be acceptable science fiction terrain. But as the novel progresses, Lewis' scientific explanations turn out to be more metaphysical than scientific, and he seems most concerned with credibly describing Malacandra and its inhabitants (elida, hrossa, and sorns). This could lead one to classify the novel as pure fantasy. But the fact that the "elida" are very similar to angels, mythic and religious parallels that are developed more fully in the sequels *Perelandra* (1943) and *That Hideous Strength* (1946), has led some to classify *Out of the Silent Planet* as a predominantly religious novel and neither "pure" science fiction nor pure fantasy. Antoine de Saint-Exupery's *The Little Prince* (1943) deals with a little boy who travels from one imaginary planet to another. But it is not a work of science fiction because its characters include a snake, a fox, a king, and a rose, and the overall effect is anecdotal and whimsical, not weighted in scientific detail. There is sometimes great debate as to whether to classify "utopian fiction" as pure fantasy or science fiction; ultimately it comes down to a decision as to whether the story is rooted in scientific plausibility or fanciful sub-creation.

Students and other readers should be aware of this problem of classification. The difference between science fiction and pure fantasy, as defined, is basic. While a story or novel might seem to overlap both sub-genres, it is usually possible to classify it successfully.

Science Fiction and Drama and Poetry

Science fiction has been defined as narrative fiction. What about the possibility of a science fiction drama or a science fiction poem?

As for science fiction drama, at least one critic has put forth a theoretical reason for saying that it cannot exist. In his essay, "On Fairy Stories," Professor Tolkien, who stresses that pure fantasy is the creation of a secondary world, contests the possibility of pure fantasy drama:

> Drama has, of its very nature, already attempted a kind of bogus, or shall I say at least substitute magic: *the visible and audible presentation of imaginary men in a story.* That is in itself an attempt to counterfeit the magician's wand. To introduce, even with mechanical success, into this quasi-magical secondary world a further fantasy or magic is to demand, as it were, an inner or tertiary world. It is a world too much. To make such a thing may not be impossible. I have never seen it done with success. But at least it cannot be claimed as the proper mode of Drama, in which walking and talking people have been found to be the natural instruments of Art and Illusion.[10]

Now, while science fiction is not pure fantasy, while it may not require the complete sub-creation that Tolkien claims for pure fantasy, it does demand scientific verisimilitude that might not be possible in the illusionary world of the theatre. Aside from a few plays such as *R.U.R.*, *Back to Methuselah*, and *Warp*, there is not a sufficient body of such plays to warrant an argument over the possibility of science fiction drama. Similar problems occur with science fiction poetry. One can concede that a narrative poem could be science fiction, assuming that scientific plausibility was somehow maintained. While there have been some poems written about science fiction topics (such as Archibald MacLeish's "Epistle to Be Left in the Earth"), there are still very few examples of this form.

And yet, some dramas have played an important part in the history of science fiction. It is safe to say that without Čapek's conception of robots in his play *R.U.R.* (1922), Asimov's *I Robot* (1950) and the accompanying "Robot Laws" would not have come about. Bernard Shaw's play cycle *Back to Methuselah* (1922), a group of five plays dealing with the biological concept of creative evolution, has been cited as an influence on such works as C.S. Lewis' *Out of the Silent Planet* (1941) and *Perelandra* (1943),[11] Arthur C. Clarke's *Childhood's End* (1953),[12] and various works by Robert Heinlein.[13]

Attempts at science fiction drama are, therefore, an important part of the history of science fiction and any course that studies this history. These dramas and science fiction-like poems can also be useful as teaching aids, as can science fiction films, which might be viewed as an extension of drama. Further discussion of science fiction drama and films will appear in the third part of this report.

2. Science Fiction in the Classroom

During the early 1970's science fiction began to be used extensively at various grade levels and in various curricula. In 1975 it was estimated that over 200 U.S. and Canadian colleges were offering science fiction courses and that untold numbers of U.S. high schools were using science fiction in the curriculum.[1] Guidelines have been developed for teaching science fiction on the elementary level.[2] The sudden interest in science fiction for classroom use has two explanations: a) the form has proved popular with young people, and it might, therefore, motivate students to a greater interest in learning, and b) science fiction has been "discovered" as a teaching tool.

"The attraction of science fiction is more often than not extraliterary, directing the reader's attention not so much towards specifically literary experiences as towards the contemplation of possibilities and wish fulfillment."[3] Science fiction, according to many educators, is interdisciplinary by its very nature, since it covers elements of science, social relations, fantasy, popular art, religion, and many other subject fields. Research and/or curriculum projects utilizing science fiction have been initiated to teach various disciplines including education,[4] science,[5] linguistics,[6] semantics,[7] world history,[8] social studies,[9] and current social issues.[10]

Science fiction has been especially valuable in education in open classroom situations—classrooms that are "open" to the world, to the future, to the individual.[11] It has been argued that science fiction, because it is interdisciplinary, because it utilizes mythic characteristics and because it represents mastery over time and space, links the past, the present, and the future.[12] It has indeed been called the basis for all future curricula. Of special interest to educators is science fiction's use of "what if"—the supposed starting point of the story in the author's mind and the premise that is used to involve the reader in the story. The question, "what if," stemming from a science fiction story, in an open classroom or any classroom situation, can engender discussion for the appropriate subject field and enable the student to express his or her views individually.

Alvin Toffler in *Future Shock*, and more extensively in *Learning for Tomorrow*, sums up the current attitude to the use of science fiction in education:

> We do not have a literature *of* the future for use in these courses, but we do have literature *about* the future, consisting not only of the great utopias but also of contemporary science fiction. Science fiction is held in low regard as a branch of literature, and perhaps it deserves this critical contempt. But if we view it as a kind of sociology of the future, rather than as literature, science fiction has immense value as a mind-stretching force for the creation of the habit of anticipation. Our children should be studying Arthur C. Clarke, William Tenn, Robert Heinlein, Ray Bradbury and Robert Sheckley, not because these writers can tell them about rocket ships and time machines but, more important, because they can lead young minds through an imaginative exploration of the jungle of political, social, psychological, and ethical issues that will confront these children as adults.[13]

It is indicative of the breadth and scope of science fiction that it can be adapted for use in so many educational disciplines. To study science fiction as social studies is not necessarily to study it as a literary form. Many of the anthologies that have been published recently in the wave of interest in science fiction purport to be designed for literature courses. But one can tell from section groupings such as "About Now," "About War," "Holocausts," "Population Problems," that the orientation of these anthologies is more toward social issues than toward a demonstration of artistic form. It is a question of focus. The same work can be discussed from many different points of view. And with each change of focus, from social concerns to philosophy to literary form, there arise different values and different criteria for judging a particular work. For teachers of literature a problem may occur when a story is admired or not admired as literature for the wrong reasons. This is not to say that to study a short story for its philosophical or sociological content is educationally wrong or wasteful, or that philosophy and the social sciences can be entirely separated from literature. But the literary dimension is at times very complex, since it deals with the interaction of form and content. Although the criteria for judging a work as literature are different from those necessary for judging a work as philosophy or sociology, they are not always mutually exclusive. In order to study science fiction as literature, there are, however, specific formal values and criteria that must be brought to bear on the work being studied.

Reasons for Teaching Science Fiction as Literature

In reading, the reader must discriminate among the different focuses that can be brought to bear on a work of literature. If the focus is philosophical, appropriate for a work of philosophy or a work with philosophical overtones, then the value with which one will judge the quality of the work is the *true*. If the focus is ethical, then the value with which one will judge the quality of the work is the *good*. If the focus is rhetorical, the value is *eloquence*. If the focus is aesthetic, if the work is to be judged primarily as literature, then the value is the *beautiful* and the criteria for judgment is *fitness*. A work is judged as literature for the way its components, its form and content, blend into one entity that is an end in itself, a thing of beauty.

A work of literature, a work of high aesthetic quality, true poetic speech, or however one wishes to define the optimum result of literary production, is an end in itself not a means to an end. It is discourse detached from the process of daily social communication.

And so, a single work can have many different qualities (philosophical, rhetorical, sociological) and it can be viewed from a focus so as to highlight a specific quality. One can read *The Time Machine* for social comments. One can read Walter M. Miller's "A Canticle for Leibowitz" or Arthur C. Clarke's "The Star" for religious insight. And consequently it is possible to read and judge by literary criteria any work of science fiction.

The question still remains, why teach science fiction as literature?

Reactions against teaching science fiction as literature stem from its jumbled history. True, antecedents of science fiction include the writings of some great literary figures and some notable works. It is also true that Verne and Wells, the genre's pathfinders in the late 19th century, were well received in the literary world. But into the 20th century there occurred the eclipse of science fiction as serious literature. The main factor in this eclipse was the emergence of science fiction magazines. The magazines were very important to the growth of science fiction in that they led to the establishment of an overall philosophy, to the development of types, motifs, and standard plots. They were also a drawback in that many of the science fiction stories in these magazines were quickly and crudely written.[14] The justification has been offered that science fiction had to dwell in these magazines in order to exist at all. Unfortunately, these all-fiction issues ate up contributions at a rapid rate and, consequently, any available material—good or bad—was included. The writers were paid little, a fact which resulted in the publication of work by hack writers who wrote quickly and jumped from magazine to magazine.[15] The label of poor quality has stuck with science fiction, even today, and even among those people, like Toffler, who support science fiction for use in education.

But there are good reasons for teaching science fiction as literature. First and foremost, it is a specific literary (sub-)genre that can be used to motivate students to an interest in literature. It can be defined easily; specific works can be used as examples. Second, it is a form in which many writers of the first rank have produced excellent work. The following is a list of writers, more or less noteworthy in other genres, who wrote antecedents of science fiction, or works that have science fiction characteristics (e.g., space travel, time travel, remarkable inventions), or works that fall within the definition of science fiction:

Lucian—*True History*, c.160 A.D.

Geoffrey Chaucer—"The Squire's Tale" in *The Canterbury Tales*, 1385–1400

Thomas More—*Utopia*, 1516

Ben Jonson—*News From the New World Discovered in the Moon*, 1621

Francis Bacon—*New Atlantis*, 1624

Daniel Defoe—*The Consolidator; Or Memoirs of Sundry Transactions from the World in the Moon. Translated from the Lunar Language*, 1705. *A Second and More Strange Voyage to the World in the Moon Containing a Comical Description of that Remarkable Country*, 1705

Jonathan Swift—*Gulliver's Travels*, 1726

Voltaire—"Micromegas," 1752

Henry Fielding—*A Journey from This World to the Next*, 1783

Edgar Allan Poe—"The Unparalleled Adventure of Hans Phall," 1835

Nathaniel Hawthorne, "Dr. Heidegger's Experiment," 1837

Herman Melville, "The Bell Tower," in *The Piazza Tales*, 1856

Edward Everett Hale, "The Brick Moon," 1870–1

Edward Bulwer-Lytton, *The Coming Race*, 1871

Oliver Wendell Holmes—*A Mortal Antipathy*, 1884

Guy de Maupassant—"The Horla," 1887

Robert Louis Stevenson—*The Strange Case of Dr. Jekyll and Mr. Hyde*, 1888

Arthur Conan Doyle—"The Los Amigos Fiasco," 1892
"The Terror of Blue John Gap," 1910
The Poison Belt, 1913
"Horror of the Heights," 1913
The Land of the Mist, 1925
"The Maracot Deep," 1927

H. G. Wells—"The Disintegrating Machine," 1929
"When the World Screamed," 1929

William Dean Howells—*Between the Dark and the Daylight* (Collection), 1907

E. M. Forster, "The Machine Stops," 1909

Jack London—"The Scarlet Plague," 1912
The Jacket (also called *The Star Rover*), 1915

Henry James—*The Sense of the Past*, 1917

F. Scott Fitzgerald—"The Curious Case of Benjamin Button" in *Flappers and Philosophers*, 1920

Karl Čapek—*R.U.R.* (Play), 1921
The Insect (Play), 1922
Land of Many Names (Play), 1923
Krakatit (Novel), 1924
Adam the Creator (Play), 1927

George Bernard Shaw—*Back to Methuselah* (Play), 1922
Farfetched Fables (Play), 1949

Stephen Vincent Benet—"The Place of the Gods" (or "By the Waters of Babylon") in *The Selected Works of Stephen Vincent Benet*, 1937

C. S. Lewis—*Out of the Silent Planet*, 1941
Perelandra, 1943
That Hideous Strength, 1946

Gore Vidal—*Messiah* (Novel), 1954
Visit to a Small Planet (TV play and play), 1955, 1957

The list is far from complete. In addition to these authors, there are writers of science fiction whose works have been well received in serious literary criticism, among them, Ray Bradbury, Arthur C. Clarke, and Robert Heinlein.

Reason three, the fact that much of science fiction magazine writing proved to be of poor quality, should not by itself disqualify the genre from serious consideration. Science fiction writer and critic Theodore Sturgeon has coined "Sturgeon's Law": ninety percent of science fiction is trash, but then ninety percent of everything is trash.[16] Also, in recent years, science fiction has come back into mainstream publishing and is demonstrating in long narrative works a range not evident in shorter magazine pieces. *Rendezvous with Rama, The Andromeda Strain, Stranger in a Strange Land, A Canticle for Liebowitz,* all were on the best-seller lists and also well received in critical circles. It has been noted that the melodrama and excessive scientific detail that dominated pulp science fiction is evident to a lesser extent in modern novels in the genre.[17]

Four, while to evaluate a science fiction story as literature is to use the criteria *fitness* alone for judgment, the fact that the genre does possess philosophical, sociological and religious aspects presents it as a literary genre of great breadth and rich texture.

Five, science fiction has been deemed by some to be worthy of serious literary evaluation because much of modern fiction is tending toward science fiction. It has been argued that science fiction eliminates the problem that has plagued fiction in the 20th century which is the failure of realism to portray things as they are.[18] This is the reason many noted novelists are now writing science fiction.[19]

Six, the emergence of science fiction as a popular phenomenon, as cult reading, is not in itself reason for studying it as literature. But it should be noted that much of science fiction's fascination comes from the mythic quality it possesses. Northrop Frye defines science fiction with reference to this quality:

> Its setting is often a kind that appears to us as technologically miraculous. It is thus a mode of romance with a strong tendency to myth.[20]

Science fiction has been known to use or extend characters from ancient myths, seemingly in the absence of similarly impressive modern characters: Adam and Eve appear in C.S. Lewis' *Perelandra,* Merlin in *That Hideous Strength,* Christ in Ray Bradbury's "The Man," the devil in Clarke's *Childhood's End.* In Robert Silverberg's "After the Myths Went Home," alterations of a time machine enable people in the year 12450 to call back all ancient myths, including Adam and Eve, Medea, Jason, Thos, Dambhala, and Pan. When their hosts become bored with them and push them back into the machine, the seeress Cassandra tells them,

> You should have kept us . . . People who have no myths of their own would do well to borrow those of others and not just as sport. Who will comfort your souls in the dark times ahead? Who will guide your spirits when the suffering begins?[21]

Science fiction stories have concerned religious and mythic situations: in Arthur C. Clarke's "The Nine Billion Names for God," the tabulation of all the names for God turns out to be the goal of existence, and at the end of the story the stars begin to go out. In Clarke's "The Sentinel" and the later extension of the original story's ideas into screenplay (and novel form), *2001: A Space Odyssey*, there are posited superior beings—or one being—whose influence is over all time and who assumes the place of godhead. Christ-figures abound in science fiction, from Ransom in *That Hideous Strength* to Smith in *Stranger in a Strange Land*.

But the mythic quality of science fiction does not stem just from its use of myth but also from its substitution *as* myth. Olaf Stapledon, in the preface to *Last and First Men* in 1930, proclaimed this intent:

> Yet our aim is not merely to create aesthetically admirable fiction. We must achieve neither mere history, nor mere fiction, but myth. A true myth is one which, within the universe of a certain culture (living or dead), expresses richly, and often perhaps tragically, the highest admirations possible within that culture. [22]

Modern people have no vital mythology as did the Greeks. The supremacy of the Judeo-Christian philosophy in western people's lives is not what it once was. The authority of science fiction as myth exists in its roots in modern science. [23] In the absence of myth or religion, people have instead found solace in fictional science that paints unknown futures where exists the imagined achievement of their waking dreams. And science fiction does fulfill a function one associates with myth: it fills the reader with a sense of wonder and awe. Its confines are the past, the present, and the future, its base is science, its premise is "what if," and its path, the path of imagination.

Perhaps what attracts people to science fiction as a substitute for myth and religion is its overall optimistic tone. It has portrayed future holocausts, but predominantly science fiction shows positive action and hope because people are people and can think and act. In Frederick Brown's "Arena," a single man pitted in combat against an alien saves the earth from destruction. "It is enough for me that there is a beyond," Lilith cries in the last line of Shaw's *Back to Methuselah*. [24] "It is this—or that: all the world or nothing? Which shall it be, Passworthy? Which shall it be?" asks John Cabel in Wells' *Things To Come*. [25] Even though the Time Traveler does not return in *The Time Machine*, even though the Invisible Man is killed in *The Invisible Man*, even though the earth team ultimately seems dwarfed by the power of the creators of Rama in *Rendezvous with Rama*, still there is wonder in the scope of the vision and a sense of hope in the mind of the reader because humanity has, if only for a moment or two, or in some small way against overpowering forces, accomplished something and is capable of doing so again and again. Although not an organized system of beliefs or tales, science fiction as a substitute for modern myth is a hymn of faith in the power of humanity.

Now this mythic quality of science fiction is not extraliterary. Mythic origins and characteristics have always been a literary consideration. Frye defines science fiction as a type of literature in relation to myth. And as for science fiction as myth, this is worthy of consideration in evaluating a work of science fiction as literature, in assessing the fitness of its parts, because this is the type of work *it is*. As James Blish claims in the title of one of his articles, science fiction is "a tale that wags the gods."

Reason seven for teaching science fiction as literature has to do with the criteria of *fitness*. A science fiction writer has a job that may be harder than that of most writers. All writers create what does not exist. A science fiction writer must create and make believable an imaginary world, a world that often has absolutely nothing in common with the real world, and he or she must create this world within a scientific reference. An educator who has any reticence about teaching science fiction as literature must realize that good science fiction, science fiction that works, presents concise characterization and exact details, and blends its components so as to make what otherwise would be an unbelievable world believable to the reader. Many science fiction works meet the criteria of *fitness*.

3. Methods of Teaching Science Fiction as Literature

Each work of science fiction must be judged individually. It is harsh generalizations about science fiction as a whole that have led to its literary eclipse. But since this report cannot evaluate *all* science fiction, it does seem appropriate to make some generalizations—if only to offset past harsh generalizations.

Style

Critics have labeled science fiction "crudely written." And, as indicated earlier, one can imagine what these critics are getting at. The usual idea of science fiction style is that which is overwritten and awkwardly phrased, such as these paragraphs from Frederick Brown's "Arena" (1943):

> He shuddered as he looked at the thing. It was alien, utterly alien, horribly different from anything on Earth or any of the life forms found on the other solar planets. Instinctively, somehow, he knew its mind was as alien as its body.
>
> But he had to try. If it had no telepathic powers at all, the attempt was foredoomed to failure, yet he thought that it had such powers. . . .
>
> For a moment that seemed an eternity he had to struggle against the mental impact of that hatred, fight to clear his mind of it and drive out the alien thoughts to which he had given admittance by blanking out his own thoughts. He wanted to retch.[1]

Also, the antiquated style of some science fiction, especially that of the 1930's, has often been criticized. An example can be found in the opening paragraph of H.P. Lovecraft's "The Shadow Out of Time" (1936):

> After twenty-two years of nightmare and terror, saved only by a desperate conviction of the mythical source of certain impressions, I am unwilling to vouch for the truth of that which I think I found in Western Australia in the night of July 17–18, 1935. There is reason to hope that my experience was wholly or partly an hallucination—for which, indeed, abundant causes existed. And yet, its realism was so hideous that I sometimes find hope impossible.[2]

Such writing may be found offensive today on the grounds that it seems pompous, archaic, and gimmicky. And yet, if one stays with the Lovecraft story, for example, one finds a fascinating tale of the exchange of the bodies of a professor of economics and a member of the "Great Race" of some age long past. This is not to say that we should excuse the stylistic faults of science fiction. The criterion for judging a work as literature is *fitness*, period. But does an antiquated style necessarily cancel out an entire work? It is a fact that the hyperbolic style of Lovecraft's opening paragraph was in keeping with the style of the times and of the science fiction magazine for which the story was written (*Astounding*). Although the reader should not excuse an overwritten style, perhaps it can be tolerated. Also, the rather hysterical tone of the passage from the Lovecraft story is fitting for a person who has recently exchanged bodies with an alien.

Nor is all science fiction written in the florid style of Lovecraft's "The Shadow Out of Time." John Wyndham's *The Midwich Cuckoos* (1957) has a similar suspense-gimmick beginning, but the style is much simpler; the voice of the narrator is reasoned, sophisticated, and obviously knowledgeable about the events of the story:

> One of the luckiest accidents in my wife's life is that she happened to marry a man who was born on the 26th of September. But for that, we should both of us undoubtedly have been at home in Midwich on the night of the 26th-27th with consequences which, I have never ceased to be thankful, she was spared.[3]

Robert Heinlein's "The Year of the Jackpot" (1971) begins in short, straightforwardly descriptive sentences which help set up an unusual situation within a realistic contemporary scene:

> At first Potiphar Breen did not notice the girl who was undressing. She was standing at a bus stop only ten feet away. He was indoors

but that would not have kept him from noticing; he was seated in a drugstore booth adjacent to the bus stop; there was nothing between Potiphar and the young lady but plate glass and an occasional pedestrian.[4]

In short, one should not make or accept generalizations about the style of science fiction writing. The style will vary depending on the author, the style of the times, and the dictates of the work itself.

Often, rather than being crudely written, some science fiction stories are rich and varied in expression. Mary S. Weinkauf has pointed out that science fiction presents a perfect example for the English classroom of such abstract concepts as verisimilitude.[5] While a Hemingway can describe postwar Paris, a science fiction writer must use language to describe what has never been. Consequently, literary devices often used in science fiction are similes (direct comparisons) and metaphors (implied comparisons). Technically, an entire science fiction story can be called a metaphor. Darko Suvin writes,

> The aliens—utopians, monsters or simply differing strangers—are a mirror to man just as the differing country is a mirror for his world.[6]

Often a sequence or event becomes a metaphor. Jimmy Pak's "Dragonfly" mechanism in Clarke's *Rendezvous with Rama* is treated as a futuristic descendant of the bicycle. The young man's exploration of the alien spaceship Rama on this "Dragonfly" provides, then, interesting comparisons of future and present inventions, ingenuity, strength, and sense of adventure. And, of course, in its descriptions, a science fiction story will employ the more common conceptions of similes and metaphors—as solitary figures of speech. This passage from Ray Bradbury's *The Martian Chronicles* demonstrates uses of both similes and metaphors to describe a land that does not and could not exist:

> It was an evening in summer upon the placid and temperate planet Mars. Up and down green wine canals, boats as delicate as bronze flowers drifted. In the long and endless dwellings that curved like tranquil snakes across the hills, lovers lay idly whispering in cool night beds. The last children ran in torchlit alleys, gold spiders in their hands throwing out films of web. Here or there a late supper was prepared in tables where lava bubbled silvery and hushed. In the ampitheatres of a hundred towns on the night side of Mars the brown Martian people with gold coin eyes were leisurely met to fix their attention upon stages where musicians made a serene music flow up like blossom scent on the still air.[7]

Characterization and Plot

It has become common for writers and critics to toss off science fiction as "a system of ideas"[8] and, consequently, a genre in which ideas are dominant over plot and character. The answer to such a statement is, what is necessarily wrong with that? Satire, for example, is primarily concerned with ideas. It would not be satire if it were not. Similarly, science fiction, since it is by definition framed within a scientific reference, is concerned with "ideas." This is not in itself a flaw. If, however, a particular story spends so much time with scientific concepts that the characters are weak and the plot is illogical, then *that* is a flaw. But if the story is dominated by science and concisely though quickly develops well-rounded characters and a believable plot, if it is able to develop some balance of these three elements within itself (again, the criterion *fitness*), then there is nothing wrong.

Characterization in science fiction is often not excessively detailed. Take, for example, H.G. Wells' *The Time Machine* (1895). Most of the characters do not even have names. They are the Time Traveler, the Medical Man, the Editor, the Journalist, and the Psychologist. But what is the advantage of giving the Time Traveler a name? The lack of a name helps build a mysterious aura around the man who can conquer time. Wells is characterizing these men by what they do. And as far as their existence in the story goes, which involves several debates about the possibility of time travel, what they do affects how they think; in other words, what they do is what they are. In Wells' *The War of the Worlds* (1898), we have it again: characters named the Curate, the Philosopher, the Artilleryman. And they are characterized by what they do, how they act, and what they talk about in the wake of destruction brought on by the Martian invaders. A reason for this characterization by title and present action is that in this time of chaos, as the world is being destroyed, this is all the first-person narrator *knows* of these people.

To take a more modern example, Captain Norton in Clarke's *Rendezvous with Rama* is described simply as "cautious." But the details pile up: his resourcefulness, his concern for his men. He is well-informed: as he boards the "Rama," he compares himself to the Egyptologist who first opened the tomb of Tutankhamen. Norton has two wives and dictates the same letter to both; yet he spares them excessive details so that they will not worry. He once had a brief affair with his surgeon Commander Laura Ernst, but forsakes the relationship as a triviality during the expedition.

However, after the rendezvous with Rama is over, with all its cosmic implications, he drifts weightless and weary in Laura's embrace. The characterization of Captain Norton could have been quite standard, but it becomes just complex enough to prove interesting and valid.

Although plot structure in science fiction is often episodic, the jumbled, episodic quality of much science fiction is not necessarily unintentional. Heinlein's *Stranger in a Strange Land,* Clarke's *2001: A Space Odyssey* and *Childhood's End,* Wells' *The Time Machine* (of course, since it proceeds in leaps of millions of years into the future), and many other science fiction works utilize the mastery of time and space presumed in the genre. Plots, then, may take the form of strings of selected episodes from the great earth-shaping events the stories depict.

To put it simply, to palm off all science fiction as something in which characterization and plot are weak because ideas are prominent is to do the genre an injustice.

Course Structure

There are several ways to organize a course on science fiction. Among these approaches are a) historical development, b) major author, c) type, and d) selective. The following course outlines for each of these methods are model guidelines only. For other student reading selections, the teacher is referred to the various listings of science fiction works, including John R. Pfeiffer's *Fantasy and Science Fiction: A Critical Guide* and Suzanne Millies' *Science Fiction Primer for Teachers.* The course outlines, generally appropriate for junior high through freshman college level, are deliberately not based on a lecture-assignment format out of the belief that since science fiction is a genre so suitable for discussion purposes there should be as little "lecturing" as possible. The outlines primarily contain reading and suggestions for teaching aids. They are intended to be followed selectively depending on the time available to the classroom group. The method of presentation, then, will vary for each grade level. The works have been selected on the basis of their literary quality and exemplification of the sub-genre, science fiction.

a) Historical Development Approach

The course will trace the literary development of science fiction from its early origins to the present day. There will, of course, be more time devoted to the works of major authors than to other writers; but the course differs from the major author approach in that developmental works, a sample of non-science fiction writers' experimentations in the form, and shorter works from science fiction magazines of the thirties and forties will be included as well.

DEFINITION: Science Fiction

Lucian, *True History*, c. 160 A.D.

Ben Jonson, *News from the New World Discovered in the Moon*, 1621

Cyrano de Bergerac, *A Voyage to the Moon*, 1650 (in *Masterpieces of Science Fiction*, ed. Sam Moskowitz, Wesport, Conn.: Hyperion Press, 1974)

Mary Wollstonecraft Shelley, "The Mortal Immortal," 1834 (in *Masterpieces of Science Fiction*)

(Possible teaching aid: George Melies' *Voyage to the Moon*, a silent film made in 1902, which typifies early science fiction films just as the above works typify early science fiction.)

Jules Verne, *A Journey to the Center of the Earth*, 1864 (Baltimore: Penguin, 1965, pap.)

Jules Verne, *Twenty Thousand Leagues Under the Sea*, 1870 (New York: E. P. Dutton and Co., 1972, pap.)

Robert Louis Stevenson, "The Strange Case of Dr. Jekyll and Mr. Hyde," 1886 (New York: Washington Square Press, 1972, pap.)

H.G. Wells, *The Time Machine*, 1895 (with *The War of the Worlds*, Greenwich, Conn.: Fawcett, 1968, pap.)

H.G. Wells, "The Star," 1897 (in *Tomorrow, and Tomorrow, and Tomorrow*, ed. Frank Herbert and others, New York: Holt, Rinehart and Winston, Inc. 1974, pap.)

(Possible teaching aid: color film, "Plot in Science Fiction," University of Kansas, 23 min.)

Arthur Conan Doyle, "The Marcot Deep," 1929 (in *the Marcot Deep*, Derby, Conn.: Belmont Tower Books, pap.)

Olaf Stapledon, *Last and First Men*, 1930 (Baltimore: Penguin, 1971)

H.P. Lovecraft, "The Shadow Out of Time," 1936 (in *The Colour Out of Space*, New York: Lancer, 1963, pap.)

(Possible teaching aid: color film, "Science Fiction: 1938 to Present," University of Kansas. Issac Asimov lectures on the origin and development of science fiction. 23 min.)

Isaac Asimov, "Nightfall," 1941 (in *Tomorrow, and Tomorrow, and Tomorrow*)

Frederick Brown, "Arena," 1944 (in *Tomorrow, and Tomorrow, and Tomorrow*)

(Possible teaching aid: feature film, *Destination Moon*, 1950, 91 min., b/w, available from St. Paul Films, 7050 Pinehurst, Dearborn, Mich., 48126. One of the earliest and best science fiction films of the 50's, typical of the times.)

Isaac Asimov, *I, Robot*, 1950 (Greenwich, Conn.: Fawcett, 1970, pap.)
Ray Bradbury, "Zero Hour," 1950 (in *The Illustrated Man*, New York:
Bantam, 1971, pap.)

(Review: "Science Fiction: Jules Verne to Ray Bradbury," a slide-tape
package from the Center for Humanities, Inc., Two Holland Avenue,
White Plains, New York, 10603)

Robert Heinlein, "The Year of the Jackpot," 1970 (in *Nightmare Age*, ed.
Frederick Pohl, New York: Ballantine, 1970, pap.)
Robert Silverberg, "After the Myths Went Home," 1971 (in *Tomorrow,
and Tomorrow, and Tomorrow*)

(Possible teaching aid: color film, "New Directions in Science Fiction,"
University of Kansas. Lecture by novelist H. Ellison on new elements in
science fiction novels. 20 min.)

Poul Anderson, "The Queen of Air and Darkness," 1971 (in *Nebula Award
Stories Seven*, ed. Lloyd Biggle, New York: Harper and Row, 1973)
Arthur C. Clarke, *Rendezvous with Rama* (New York: Ballantine, 1973,
pap.)

b) Major Authors Approach

After a brief discussion of what science fiction is, the course will center
on major authors of science fiction and their work.

DEFINITION: Science Fiction
Summary of development of science fiction to Verne

Jules Verne
Journey to the Center of the Earth, 1864
Twenty Thousand Leagues Under the Sea, 1870

H.G. Wells
The Time Machine, 1895, *The War of the Worlds*, 1898 (Greenwich, Conn.:
Fawcett, 1968, pap.)
"The Star," 1897
The Invisible Man, 1897 (New York: Berkeley, pap.)
Things To Come (Screenplay in narrative form. New York: Macmillan,
1935)
(Possible teaching aids:
film, "H.G. Wells, Man of Science," Indiana A.V. Center, b/w, 30 min.
film, "Whoosh: An Outline of H.G. Wells," Time-Life, b/w, 35 min.)

Olaf Stapledon
Last and First Men, 1930

Isaac Asimov
"Nightfall," 1941
I, Robot, 1950
The Foundation Trilogy, 1951—3 novels (New York: Avon, 1974, pap.)

Ray Bradbury
"Zero Hour," 1950
The Martian Chronicles, 1950 (New York: Bantam, 1970, pap.)
Fahrenheit 451, 1953 (New York: Ballantine, 1972, pap.)

Arthur C. Clarke
"The Sentinel"
"The Nine Billion Names for God," 1954 (in *Science Fiction Hall of Fame*,
    ed. Robert Silverberg, New York: Avon, 1972, pap.)
Childhood's End (New York: Ballantine, 1970, pap.)
2001: A Space Odyssey (New York: NAL, Signet, 1972, pap.)

(Possible teaching aid: *2001: A Space Odyssey*, a feature film directed by
Stanley Kubrick from a screenplay by Clarke and Kubrick. The film,
partially derived from "The Sentinel," was the basis for Clarke's book of
the same name, and is a summation of much of Clarke's writings.)

Kurt Vonnegut
The Sirens of Titan, 1960 (New York: Dell, 1971, pap.)
Cat's Cradle, 1964 (New York: Dell, 1970, pap.)
Slaughterhouse Five, 1969 (New York: Dell, 1971, pap.)

(Possible teaching aid: *Vonnegut Space Fantasy—Between Time and
Timbuktu*, Public Broadcasting Service, 1972. Available from New Line
Cinema, 121 University Place, New York, New York, 10003)

c) **Approach by Type**

In this approach, science fiction will be taught by various types of
stories. It has an advantage that the other methods do not have in
that it demonstrates to the student the many different kinds of
stories that can fall under the definition *science fiction*.

C.S. Lewis divides science fiction into five sub-species: a) those
that leap a thousand years to find plots and passions they could have
found at home; b) "the fiction of engineers" which is primarily
interested in space travel; c) scientific but speculative stories that
wonder "what would life be like if . . ." d) "eschatological science
fiction" which gives an imaginary vehicle to speculations about the
ultimate destiny of our species; and e) stories about gods, ghouls,
ghosts, demons, fairies—for which plausibility is not essential.[9]
Some critics go in the other direction toward minuteness. Suzanne
Millies divides science fiction into such broad headings as "Man and
Science" and under that division lists the following subheadings:
"The Control of Man's Mind;" "Inventions That Backfire;" "Com-
puters That Take Over;" "Man and the Robot;" and "The Mad-
Scientist Syndrome."[10] Donald Wollheim breaks science fiction into
the following simple list of groupings: a) imaginary voyages; b) fu-
ture prediction; c) remarkable inventions; and c) social satires.[11]
Countless other divisions have been tried.

The following list utilizes some of the types coined by Lewis, Millies and Wollheim and is simple enough for a class syllabus:

> imaginary voyages
> alien beings
> inventions or discoveries
> visions of the future
> scientific concepts (time, other dimensions, evolution)

This course outline is suggested:

DEFINITION: Science Fiction
DISCUSSION AND DEFINITION:
The various types of science fiction

Type A—Imaginary Voyages

Jules Verne, *Journey to the Center of the Earth*
Arthur C. Clarke, *Rendezvous with Rama*

(Possible teaching aids: films, *A Trip to the Moon*, 1902, *2001: A Space Odyssey*, 1968)

Type B—Alien Beings

Frederick Brown, "Arena"
Arthur C. Clarke, *Childhood's End*
H.G. Wells, *The War of the Worlds*
John Wyndham, *The Midwich Cuckoos* (New York: Walker & Co., 1957)
Alan Dean Foster, "With Friends Like These," (in the *1972 Annual World's Best Science Fiction*, Donald A. Wollheim, ed., New York: Daw Books, 1972)

(Possible teaching aid: feature film, *The Day the Earth Stood Still*, 1951, based on Harry Bates, "Farewell to the Master." Available from Films Incorporated, 425 North Michigan Ave., Chicago, Ill. 60611, with branches in Atlanta, Boston, Dallas, Hollywood, New York City, Portland, and Skokie, Ill.)

Type C—Inventions or Discoveries

H.G. Wells, *The Invisible Man*
Robert Louis Stevenson, "The Strange Case of Dr. Jekyll and Mr. Hyde"
Mary Wollstonecraft Shelley, *Frankenstein* (New York: Oxford University Press, 1971, pap.)
Daniel Keyes, "Flowers for Algernon" (in *The Hugo Winners, Vol. I*, Isaac Asimov, ed., Garden City, New York: Doubleday and Co., 1962)

(Possible teaching aid: feature film, *Charley*, 1968, based on "Flowers for Algernon," 103 min. Available from Films Incorporated.)

Type D—Visions of the Future

Pierre Boulle, *Planet of the Apes* (New York: NAL, Signet, 1968, pap.)
Robert A. Heinlein, "The Year of the Jackpot"

Aldous Huxley, *Brave New World* (New York: Harper & Row, pap.)
Frank Herbert, *Dune* (New York: Ace, 1965, pap.)
Anthony Burgess, *A Clockwork Orange* (New York: Ballantine, 1971, pap.)
(Possible teaching aid: feature film, *Planet of the Apes*, 1968, from the Boulle novel. Available from Films Incorporated)

Type E—Scientific Concepts

H.G. Wells, *The Time Machine*
Edwin A. Abbott, *Flatlands* (New York: Dover, 1952)
Kurt Vonnegut, *Slaughterhouse Five* (New York: Dell, 1971, pap.)

d) Selective

This method of teaching science fiction relies on the use of *quality* science fiction, science fiction worthy of the name *literature*. All works selected should demonstrate *fitness*. It should be remembered, however, since this is a course in science fiction, that all works studied should conform to a definition of science fiction and even prove exemplary of the sub-genre. This method places great responsibility on the selection skills of the instructor. A suggested outline follows:

DEFINITION: Science Fiction
DEFINITION: Literature

H.G. Wells, "The Star"
H.G. Wells, *The War of the Worlds*
Ray Bradbury, "Zero Hour"
Ray Bradbury, *The Martian Chronicles*
Poul Anderson, "The Queen of Air and Darkness"
Frank Herbert, *Dune*
Aldous Huxley, *Brave New World*
Robert Silverberg, "After the Myths Went Home"
Olaf Stapledon, *Last and First Men*
Walter M. Miller, "A Canticle for Leibowitz"
Ursula K. LeGuin, *The Left Hand of Darkness*

Four Examples

In order to provide examples of how science fiction can be taught as literature, four science fiction works are analyzed: three short stories and one novel. The first story, "Zero Hour," is the most appropriate of the four for elementary grades and is analyzed accordingly. The criteria for judgment in all cases is that of *fitness.* Each analysis provides points that should be included in both the teacher's own preparation and in the actual classroom discussion.

A good place to begin in analyzing a story or novel as literature is the opening paragraph or section, which often determines the work's structure, focus, plot and method of characterization. Ask students to determine the voice (first person, third person, third person omniscient, descriptive, satirical). The voice is often a unifying and structuring element in a work. Encourage students to see if there are patterns in the language or in the themes. Are the characters well-rounded? Is the action of the work logical? Finally, do all of the various elements blend? Does the work demonstrate *fitness?* Are there enough patterns and interrelations to make it a consciously wrought entity and end in itself?

"Zero Hour" by *Ray Bradbury* (from *The Illustrated Man*)

Synopsis: In the course of a day, Mink runs in and out telling her mother, Mrs. Morris, about a new game she and the other children are playing called "Invasion." Mink says the children are playing the game with Drill, a being from another planet who is working only with the children of the earth because they are "impressionable." "Zero Hour," Mink claims, is set for five o'clock. Mrs. Morris pays little attention to Mink. At five o'clock, soon after Mr. Morris comes home, there is an explosion. Mr. and Mrs. Morris seek safety in the attic, only to be pursued there by Mink who is followed by "tall blue shadows."

The story begins,

Oh, it was to be so jolly! What a game! Such excitement they hadn't known in years. The children catapulted this way and that across the green lawns, shouting at each other, holding hands, flying in circles, climbing trees, laughing. Overhead the rockets flew, and the beetle cars whispered by on the streets, but the children played on. Such fun, such tremulous joy, such tumbling and hearty screaming.

33

In this opening paragraph, it is established that the story is to be about children. The voice appropriately uses short, simple sentences, reflecting the shouts and manner of the children. It is not a child's voice, though, as such constructions as "hearty screaming" attest. It is a descriptive voice that reflects the children's joy.

The opening paragraph also establishes that the story is set in the future (the reference to rockets). There is also the early indication of a difference between the naive, carefree world of the children and the busy, unheeding world of adults. This is continued in the second paragraph where it is said Mrs. Morris "hardly saw" Mink when the child entered looking for tools. It is a major point of the story that Mrs. Morris could learn from Mink what is going on (as the reader surely does) if she only listened to her daughter.

Although there is a voice framing the story, a voice using simple language reflecting and blending with the language of the little girl Mink, "Zero Hour" is told mostly in dialogue between Mrs. Morris and Mink. The use of dialogue is effective as it allows the reader to gradually obtain information about the "game" and also because it highlights Mrs. Morris' inability to communicate with her child:

> "Who's invading what?"
> "Martians invading Earth. Well, not exactly Martians. They're—I don't know. From up." She pointed with her spoon.
> "And *inside*," said Mom, touching Mink's feverish brow.
> Mink rebelled. "You're laughing! You'll kill Drill and *every*body."
> "I didn't mean to," said Mom. "Drill's a Martian?"
> "No. He's—well—maybe from Jupiter or Saturn or Venus. Anyway, he's had a hard time."
> "I imagine." Mrs. Morris hid her mouth behind her hand.
> "They couldn't figure a way to attack Earth."
> "We're impregnable," said Mom in mock seriousness.
> "That's the word Drill used! Impreg— That was the word, Mom."

The growth of awareness of both the reader and, eventually, Mrs. Morris as to exactly what is happening, as can be gleaned from the dialogue, is a unifying element of this story. Bit by bit the reader hears of the game "Invasion," Mink using words outside of her vocabulary, Drill—a being from another planet whom the children are trying to help enter from another dimension, Mink's possession of a yo-yo that disappears, and an audio-visor call from Mrs. Morris' friend Helen in New York in which Helen claims that her children are playing with Drill, as are children around the country.

The theme of a generation gap is also a unifying element. The theme is constantly repeated as Mink quotes Drill's creed of dealing only with children because parents know too much and are, therefore, "dangerous." Drill's methods suit the latent instincts of the children who shun "crybabies," older children who make fun of them, and grown-ups who do not understand them. The children are never portrayed as vicious, however, but merely as children who do not realize they are destroying the world. The last line of the story, Mink's greeting to her parents as she opens the door with the aliens behind her, is that of a child: "Peakaboo."

The story meets the definition of science fiction: it is a prose narrative dealing with events that cannot happen at the present time couched within scientific or at least pseudo-scientific concepts (other dimensions, life on other planets or in other dimensions). It displays *fitness*. It is unified by the framing voice that reflects the simple style of the children the story is about, by the growth of understanding of Mrs. Morris and the readers of what is happening, and the theme of a generation gap (a lack of understanding between parents and children).

Teaching Suggestions

The story is especially suitable for the upper elementary and junior high schools as it is simple in style and content and deals with something most children are very aware of—the difference in understanding of children and adults. Here are some ideas for getting students involved in the story:

• Discussion of the generation gap, its credibility as expressed in the story, and its dangers in terms of the story. Guide questions—Why didn't Mrs. Morris listen? Why didn't any of the mothers across the country listen? Do parents listen? Can you point out passages in the dialogue where Mrs. Morris should have been listening and wasn't?

• A written paragraph or short essay about what the tall blue shadows look like as suggested in the story. (The students might even be asked to draw their idea of what the aliens look like. This might help them conceptualize the story.)

• Discussion and/or essay about the credibility of the scientific aspects of the story (audio-visor, etc.) Guide questions—What do the new devices look like? How are they like equipment we have today? How are they different?

• Discussion and/or essay about the way Mink talks. Guide question—Do children really talk like that? This might be developed into a dramatic activity with student performers that could be audiotaped.

"The Star" by *H. G. Wells*

Synopsis: The story describes the effects of a star coming very close to colliding with the earth. Much of the earth is destroyed. But from the point of view of Martian astronomers little damage is done considering the size of the star.

The story begins in this way:

> It was on the first day of the new year that the announcement was made, almost simultaneously from three observatories, that the motion of the planet Neptune, the outermost of all the planets that wheel about the sun, had become very erratic. Ogilvy had already called attention to a suspected retardation in its velocity in December. Such a piece of news was scarcely calculated to interest a world the greater portion of whose inhabitants were unaware of the existence of the planet Neptune, nor outside of the astronomical profession did the subsequent discovery of a faint remote speck of light in the region of the perturbed planet cause any great excitement.

The star appears, appropriately and forbiddingly enough, on the first day of the new year. Efforts at some passing scientific credibility are apparent in the fact that the sighting was confirmed by three observatories at once, by reference to the orbit of Neptune, and reference to Ogilvy as a noted authority. The third sentence demonstrates the approach of the story: focusing on the reaction of people and the earth in general to the star. At first, the interest in the star is confined to scientists. But as the star becomes more and more visible, the world takes notice.

The voice of the narrator is third person omniscient. It primarily reports. But that third sentence indicates that it is a knowledgeable voice; it knows that most of the world couldn't care less about stars and planets. This voice is, therefore, able to perceive irony in a situation:

> By the second day it was clearly visible to any decent instrument, as a speck with a barely sensible diameter, in the constellation Leo near Regulus. In a little while an opera glass could attain it.

It is an omniscient voice and detached from the action, though it occasionally adopts an ironic tone. And it reports on *everything*. The voice describes different reactions to the star, shifting from place to place. A weeping woman kneeling beside her dead son wonders why a star should matter to her. A schoolboy uses the star as an example for studying centrifugal and centripetal force.

Different people react in different ways:

> In a South African city a great man had married, and the streets were alight to welcome his return with his bride. "Even the skies have illuminated," said the flatterer.

Two lovers who see the star from a canebrake whisper, "That's our star," and feel "comforted" by its brilliance.

The master mathematician says to the star:

> "You may kill me . . . But I can hold you—and all the universe for that matter—in the grip of this little brain. I would not change that."

He then proceeds to use the future destruction of the earth as the basis for his lecture.

Juxtaposed against this shifting of scenes to get different reactions to the star is the use of repetition to indicate, still through the reaction of people, that the star is continually getting closer:

> "It is brighter!" cried the people clustering in the streets. But in the dim observatories the watchers held their breath and peered at one another. "*It is nearer,*" they said. "*Nearer!*"
>
> And voice after voice repeated, "It is nearer," and the clicking telegraph took that up, and it trembled along telephone wires, and in a thousand cities grimy compositors fingered the type. "It is nearer." Men writing in offices, struck with a strange realization, flung down their pens, men talking in a thousand places suddenly came upon a grotesque possibility in these words, "It is nearer."

A whole pattern of repetition develops. The device of shifting scenes is repeated as the proximity of the star causes havoc on the earth. Different areas of the world are observed: Tidal waves hit the coasts and plains of China. Japan, Java, and all the islands of East Asia are full of steam, smoke and ashes from volcanoes. Storms and earthquakes spread all down America.

The scientific explanation given by the Master Mathematician is not that the star will collide with earth but that the star was attracted to the planet Jupiter's orbit, alters the course of that planet, and passes near the earth.

It might be wondered about the omniscient voice how the person survived all this destruction to tell the story. Also, how could he or she be so detached from such destruction? The answer is given by the reference to the Martian astronomers. The narrator is of the future, probably from another planet. At first, the mention of Martians might be seen as a trick ending. But the identification of the narrator as a future being is in keeping with the omniscient, detached, occasionally ironic voice of the story, and also provides an explanation for the existence of this person. The omniscient voice may even remind some readers of Spock in "Star Trek."

Characterization is brief but concise. The characters are not named and are identified by their title or types: master mathematician, two lovers, a great man. But it is appropriate characterization coming from descriptions by a future being of past people and events, seemingly observed from a great height. Also, the people are defined by their relation to the star: lovers who see it, a schoolboy who studies it, a mathematician who understands what it is, a widow who mourns her dead in its light. This is the basis for their being described at all. The star itself is almost a character: its existence and movement affects these people; the master mathematician even feels enough rapport with the star to talk to it. Of these characters, the master mathematician is the most detailed. He exemplifies courage and pride in the power of the mind, all of which speaks well of humanity. Again, we find in science fiction that even though the earth is all but destroyed, humanity, on the whole, behaves admirably.

As to the style, at first the voice merely reports what occurs in descriptive, sometimes complex, but always controlled and grammatical sentences. But as the star approaches, the style reflects the situation. Sentences become long and frantic, with no sentence breaks, detailing panicked flight and destruction, repetitive, alliterative, emphasizing "s," "h," and "m" sounds to convey a sense of speed and crowds:

> Until that wave came at last—in a blinding light and with the breath of a furnace, swift and terrible it came—a wall of water, fifty feet high, roaring hungrily, upon the long coasts of Asia, and swept inland across the plains of China. For a space the star, hotter now and larger and brighter than the sun in its strength, showed with pitiless brilliance the wide and populous country; towns and villages with their pagodas and trees, roads, wide cultivated fields, millions of sleepless people staring in helpless terror at the incandescent sky; and then, low and growing, came the murmur of the flood. And thus it was with millions of men that night—a flight nowhither, with limbs heavy with heat and breath fierce and scant and the flood like a wall swift and white behind. And then death.

"The Star" is a science fiction story: it concerns an incident of the imagined future, with a being from some future date as narrator. Scientific plausibility and scientific detail are evident. "The Star" exhibits *fitness*. Events are described and unified by an omniscient, detached, though at times ironic voice. The detached, omniscient voice dictates the structure of the story, which is composed of reactions around the world to the star. The voice also dictates brief but concise characterizations, as if glimpsed fleetingly by the narrator or people from another planet from a great height. There is a pattern of repetition in the story, not only of speech but of devices (such as the shifting of scenes). The style follows the mood of the action: at first calmly reportive, then frantically descriptive as if caught up in the destruction. Even the surprise conclusion which alludes to the existence of Martians and other alien beings is in keeping with the detached, omniscient voice.

Teaching Suggestions

Photographs and illustrations of stars, particularly comets and meteors (since these are the stars most likely to approach earth) can be brought into class to give pictoral representation to the Wells story. Students can be asked to consult an encyclopedia and other sources for descriptions of stars. Also, students can be assigned to find in books and newspapers reactions, especially panicked ones, to sightings of comets, or of UFO's, and these can be compared to the descriptions in the Wells story.

Students might be asked to write critiques comparing "The Star" with another story or film. Similar fictions about the collision of other interplanetary bodies with earth are Edgar Allan Poe's "The Conversation of Eiros and Charmion" (in the *Treasury of Science Fiction Classics,* New York: Hanover House, 1954) and Edwin Balmer and Philip Wylie's *When Worlds Collide* (1932, Paperback Library, 1973, pap.) A feature film was made of the latter in 1950. Reference can also be made to Arthur C. Clarke's *Rendezvous with Rama* (1973) in which, for a while, the unidentified space object is thought to be a collapsed star on collision course with earth; in chapter two of this book, a scientist even draws a comparison of this event with the Wells story.

Wells was primarily interested in the reaction of people to speculative events. It would, therefore, be helpful to a class in conceptualizing such events both in a general way and as they concern Wells in particular, to dramatize or have dramatized the Howard Koch/Orson Welles radio adaptation of Wells' *The War of The Worlds* (in Howard Koch's *The Panic Broadcast,* New York: Avon, 1971, pap.) A possible class project based on the radio treatment of *The War of the Worlds* would be a student dramatization of "The Star" within the context of a TV news show. The story might be updated for this, but the students should recognize and know the reasons for any changes they may make.

"The Queen of Air and Darkness"
by *Poul Anderson*

Synopsis: Barbro Cullen's child is kidnapped on the planet Roland. Barbro consults a detective, Eric Sherrinford, and together they investigate the possibility the boy was kidnapped by Outlings or Old Folk, very similar to faerie creatures of old earth lore. Barbro is captured by the Outlings, is reunited with her son, and confronts the Queen of Air and Darkness who almost makes Barbro one of them. Sherrinford rescues both Barbro and her son. At the end of the story, the Outlings appear to have been all but destroyed.

The story begins:

> The last glow of the last sunset would linger almost until midwinter. But there would be no more day, and the northlands rejoiced. Blossoms opened, flamboyance on firethorn trees, steelflowers rising blue from the brok and rainplant that cloaked all hills, shy whiteness of kiss-me-never down in the dales. Flitteries darted among them on irridescent wings; a crownbuck shook his horns and bugled. Between horizons the sky deepened from purple to sable. Both moons were aloft, nearly fully, shining frosty on leaves and molten on waters. The shadows they made were blurred by an aurora, a great blowing curtain of light across half heaven. Behind it the earliest stars had come out.

The opening paragraph is full of wonder in its description of a sunset. It is almost poetry in its use of alliteration and rhythm. It carries strange words and presents an eerie, otherworldly atmosphere. The first section of the story continues with the introduction of such characters as Mistherd, Shadow-of-a-Dream, Ayoch (a pook) and the Queen of Air and Darkness, all of whom confer over the kidnapped child. This short story is very close to pure fantasy in its use of elfin creatures and magic. It is a blending of both pure fantasy and science fiction as the earth legends of faerie creatures and changelings are transferred to outerspace. The story is an admission of humans' deep-rooted belief in legends and other nonscientific conceptions. Barbro expresses this to Sherrinford:

> ". . . Oh, I suppose it's just something left over from my outway childhood, but do you know, when I'm under them I can't think of the stars as balls of gas, whose energies have been measured, whose planets have been walked on by prosaic feet. No, they're small and cold and magical; our lives are bound to them; after we die, they whisper to our graves." Barbro glanced downward. "I realize that's nonsense."

It is interesting to compare "The Queen of Air and Darkness" with Tolkien's fantasy trilogy *The Lord of the Rings* which preceded the Anderson story. The similarities between the two works include the creation of otherworldly beings (Tolkien uses hobbits and ents, Anderson pooks, nicors, and wraiths), the use of new language and songs, and especially the reaction to the faerie worlds. Both *The Lord of the Rings* and "The Queen of Air and Darkness" exhibit admiration for these faerie worlds, but both works end with the worlds dying out because their time has come.

Anderson creates in a sense, two other worlds; a future world, the planet Roland where humanoid life has spread since "earth long ago sunk into alien concerns"; and the faerie world of the Outlings. It is better to say that it is one "other world" for, since this is predominantly science fiction (everything is couched within a scientific reference), what Anderson has done is create a scientific explanation for these Outlings that have inhabited possibly the earth and now Roland.

The planet Roland is well-documented in scientific detail. Roland's sun is called Charlemagne (type F9, forty percent brighter than Sol). It has two moons: Oliver and Alde. It is a globe 9500 kilometers in diameter which rotates once in thirty-two hours; its surface gravity is $0.42 \times 980 \text{cm/sec}^2$; the sea level pressure is slightly above one Earth atmosphere. New technology and concepts appear as Barbro cooks a meal on a "glower," Sherrinford talks to the sheriff on a "visiphone" and estimates Barbro's age in both Rolandic and Terrestrial years. But the scientific details extend even to the provision of a scientific explanation for the Outlings: they are aborigines, territorial in nature; they hide both because they are cautious of humans and because they are a species used to little direct sunlight and therefore avoid the sun; they possess mental gifts including the ability to read minds and generate hallucinations; they steal human children partly to conform to their pattern of inspiring fear and partly in order to study and experiment on members of the human species. All of this provides a rational explanation for earth tales of faeries and little people (such as the Irish faerie tales of the Shi or the Dutch ghosts in Washington Irving's "Rip Van Winkle") who could cloud men's minds with illusions and make them forget their past lives.

And so, "The Queen of Air and Darkness" contains pure fantasy elements; it belongs to the sub-genre science fiction. But in addition, it has an overall structure of a detective story. The heroine comes to a detective and asks him to find her missing child. There are questions—who stole the child, and how? are there Out-lings?—clues pile up, the heroine is captured and is rescued by the detective, his guns blazing.

In addition to the organizing structure of the detective story, the story is unified by the continued use of the theme of illusion versus reality. The story is composed of sequences which alternate between the "real" world of Barbro and Sherrinford and the "faerie" world of the Outlings. The nakedness and abandon of the Outlings in the opening sequences is contrasted with the reported troubled times that have beset human life and the unease with which some of the humans act. Barbro is captured by the Outlings when she follows the illusion of her son Jimmy. She is carried by a man who speaks in the voice of her dead husband; she also sees the dog named Sambo that she had when she was a girl. But her "hus-band" grows weak and is led away by a hooded figure; the dog vanishes. Sherrinford gets the cooperation of the young changeling Mistherd by turning off the "mind-shield" as the Outlings ap-proach, then turning it back on so that Mistherd can see them as they really are. Anderson has coralled pure fantasy and science fic-tion into one story not just as a stunt but to highlight the theme of illusion versus reality. Barbro admits a desire to believe that stars whisper to our graves after we die. Humans captured by Outlings seem to succumb readily to the charms of their existence. Chief Constable Dawson avoids the question of Outlings. William Irons and his family, who live farther out, sing the songs of the Outlings. There is a strong indication that the world has become too technical and mechanical, and that humans inwardly cling to a belief in these magic creatures who romp naked through fields and for whom noth-ing is dull or ordinary. In the "Arvid Song" that the family of William Irons sings, the Queen of Air and Darkness says to the ranger Arvid who has refused her,

> In work and play and friendship
> Your grief will strike you dumb
> For thinking what you are—and—
> What you might have become.

But in the end, many Outlings are killed by Sherrinford's guns. The Outlings disband, soon to become absorbed into humanity. The Queen of Air and Darkness is dead and Ayoch the pook sings a tribute to her before he flies away:

Out of her breast
A blossom ascended.
The summer burned it.
The song is ended.

Sherrinford adopts the common-sense attitude that it had to be done. But the song claims that "a blossom ascended" and was burned. Reality must prevail. Dreams must fade.

The characterizations are serviceable if not well-rounded. Barbro is a typical lady-in-distress with clearly delineated physical characteristics (she is a big woman of thirty, broad-shouldered, long-legged, full-breasted, supple of stride). She is a woman of science who instinctively believes in the unbelievable. Sherrinford has more to do and say: it is he who solves the mystery. He considers himself a follower in the archetype of the rational detective—Sherlock Holmes. At the end, we are led to believe that a romantic relationship has developed between these two lonely people. But even the characterization of Sherrinford is somewhat diminished as he is made to rescue Barbro in his camper bus equipped with a gun turret. Far more interesting, both because they are the key to the mystery and because of the uniqueness of finding such creatures in a science fiction tale, are the Outlings: Mistherd, the young boy changeling who becomes Sherrinford's guide; Shadow-of-a-Dream, Mistherd's female companion; Ayoch the pook (with long, clawfooted legs, a half-human face, and a body covered with feathers) who kidnaps the Cullen boy; Morgarel the wraith (telepathic); Nagrim the nicor (huge and four armed); and the Queen of Air and Darkness who stands alone in her nakedness. But even these creatures, although generally unfamiliar to the reader, claim their believability not from their existence in the story but from their relation to earth-based legends. But just as Anderson has connected his blending of science fiction and pure fantasy to the themes of illusion versus reality, so this reliance on archetypes is made to seem purposeful in a speech by Sherrinford that expounds that archetypes (his resemblance to Sherlock Homes, the Outlings' resemblance to earth legends) run through all history.

"The Queen of Air and Darkness" is a science fiction story—it concerns events and ideas not possible in daily life that are framed within a scientific reference. It is conceivable that there can be quibbling over some points. The characterization of the human characters is generally rather standard. Anderson's use of earth legends becomes very literal when he names the plant "Roland," the moons "Oliver," and "Alde" and the sun "Charlemagne." Finally, it is perhaps a tribute to the point of the story—that belief in such things as myths and legends persists even in scientific ages—that the reader is disappointed by Sherrinford's final explanation of the Outlings. Sherrinford tends to the rationale that the Outlings are not the "faerie" creatures from earth but are inhabitants of the planet Roland who adopted this guise knowing that humans feared such creatures. It is in keeping with the science fiction nature of the story that the Outlings are definitely identified as *not* faerie creatures, but this explanation seems a little forced, especially as the Outlings act like faerie creatures even when mortals are not around.

The story blends science fiction and pure fantasy; it is unified by a detective story structure and by the theme of illusion versus reality that complements the pure fantasy/science fiction nature of the story.

Teaching Suggestions

Students can be asked to trace literary antecedents of Anderson's faerie creatures. Additional reading assignments to give the students an idea of the faerie worlds Anderson is incorporating into his science fiction tale might include James Stephens' *The Crock of Gold* (1912, N.Y.: Collier, 1967, pap.) and selections from Tolkien's *The Hobbit* (1939, N.Y.: Ballantine, 1967, pap.) Further comparisons with other literature are possible, for instance the comparison of the Arvid song sung by the William Irons family with John Keats' "La Belle Dame Sans Merci." Reference can also be made to A. E. Housman's three stanza poem "Her Strong Enchantments Failing" which contains the following lines:

> The Queen of air and darkness
>   Begins to shrill and cry,
> 'O Young man, O my slayer,
>   To-morrow you shall die.'

Other assignments can include students finding or selecting readings from other fiction that combine elements of various genres with science fiction. Anderson himself has attempted similar combinations before. His "The Martian Crown Jewels" (in *Great Science Fiction Stories*, Dell, 1964) again uses a detective story framework for a science fiction story. There is even another character who is a futuristic embodiment of Sherlock Holmes; this time he is a noted Martian detective. The television series *Star Trek* featured stories that used Alice in Wonderland, Apollo, and a fallen angel as characters.

It might be interesting to undertake activities involving the language of "The Queen of Air and Darkness." Tolkien in *The Lord of the Rings* provided pronunciation keys and a glossary for languages he coined. There is not as much language invention in "The Queen of Air and Darkness" as in Tolkien. But the students could develop etymologies for coined words and place names in the story, both words used in the faerie world of the story and words from the futuristic world. Extensive vocabularies might be constructed, leading to the formulation of dictionaries.

Childhood's End by *Arthur C. Clarke*

Synopsis: In 1975, the Overlords from another planet take over the earth and bring it to perfect, though sterile, order. At first, they do not show themselves. But after fifty years, the earth is allowed to see Karellen, Supervisor for Earth—he has horns, wings, a barbed tail. In short, he is the image of the devil. Eventually, it develops that the Overlords are acting for "the Overmind" and their mission is to take away and watch over certain earth children who have developed into superior beings. The children are part of the Overmind's ultimate plan. It is through them that human life continues. But humanity as a whole dies out and the earth is destroyed in order to provide energy for the children's departing flight to join the Overmind.

The novel begins with a prologue in which the Russians and Americans are about to launch rockets to the moon only to be stopped by the arrival of the Overlords. The novel is divided into three topical divisions: a) Earth and the Overlords; b) The Golden Age; and c) The Last Generation. The novel is episodic in structure but is unified by the following principle: the continual development of understanding of the nature and mission of the Overlords. The first section, therefore, traces the relationship between Stormgren, the Secretary-General of the United Nations, and Karellen, including the kidnapping of Stormgren by anti-Overlord factions and Stormgren's attempt to get a glimpse of Karellen's face. The second section details the first appearance of the Overlords to the world, the peaking of the "Golden Age" on earth, and the plan of Jan to get to the Overlord planet. The final section describes the discovery of George and Jean Greggson that their two children are "chosen," the revelation of the mission of the Overlords, Jan's exploration of the Overlord's planet, and his return to earth as the sole surviving earthling.

The topical, episodic structure is, therefore, unified by the development of understanding of both the reader and earthlings in the novel of the nature of the Overlords. The scope of time is vast, but a pattern of human behavior emerges even though the characterizations are not detailed. Stormgren, George, Jean, Jan, Duval (the scientist who helps Stormgren see Karellen), Sullivan (the scientist who helps Jan get to the planet of the Overlords)—in short those characters who are given any appreciable space—all display a quest for knowledge and understanding of their situation. Duval and Sullivan in particular are portrayed as competent but "little" people who have never made it in a big way. It is somehow appropriate that in a novel which is basically an overview of the last hundred years of earth, these individuals—not superheroes but ordinary men and women—are the ones who play important roles. They are distinguished by a belief in the rational, a desire to know and act, and finally, by resigned acceptance. Stormgren knows that he will never see the Overlords; George, the writer, knows that humanity has lots its human future; Jean knows that she will never see her children again; and Jan knows that he will not survive long as the last man on earth. Even though the earth is destroyed and humanity is no more, the novel is not pessimistic. There is a plan to the universe; human beings just happen to play a very small part in that plan. But the humans portrayed *are* notable, and something of the nature of humanity continues, working toward the perfection of Creation, in the earth children.

The dominant and the most impressive character of the novel is Karellen. At first he is a mysterious voice who playfully calls Stormgren "Rikki" and who evidently knows everything that happens on earth. But he is the one character who is present throughout the novel and therefore the one able to develop most fully. As the novel progresses, it becomes apparent that Karellen and all the Overlords are not omnipotent, but rather, eunuchs in the evolution of the universe, fit only to serve and not to initiate action. One senses that behind Karellen's wit and aloofness is someone who wishes to be involved but can only watch—the children, the earth, seemingly now in perfect order, heading for inevitable destruction. When the mission is over, and the earth is gone, Karellen, who has watched it all with surface detachment, evidences regret and pity. He, like the other characters in the novel, is ultimately a "little person" in the vast scope and plan of the universe. But he too behaves with dignity and resigned acceptance.

Karellen appears in the image of the devil. This is one of the many Judeo-Christian images that occur throughout the novel. Jan hiding in the stuffed whale bound for the planet of the Overlords evokes the Bible story of Jonah. Jeff, the son of George and Jean, is saved from a tidal wave by a mysterious voice—like the voice that called Abraham and Noah. The earth children, who fly to the Overmind, recall the statement of Christ, "Let the children come to me and do not hinder them. It is to just such as these that the kingdom of God belongs." The chosen children first exhibit their uniqueness by their recurrent dreams; dreams are a typical means of communication between God and man in the Bible. And finally, the Overmind itself is surely some form of Godhead. There is also a pattern and repetition of motifs: ascent (the planned rocket shots of the novel's prologue, Jan's trip to the Overlord's planet, the children's flight at the end) and descent (Stormgren's prison in the underground cave, Stormgren's visit to Duval underground, Jan's descent into the belly of a whale).

The voice of the novel is third person omniscient. At first it limits itself to descriptions of humanity's reactions to the Overlords. But since the Overlords are introduced to the reader as characters in Section Two, several conversations between Overlords are described in Sections Two and Three. This omniscient voice adopts a somewhat elegiac tone appropriately enough, toward the end of the novel as the earth is destroyed.

There are flaws in the novel. The fact that Clarke has chosen a structure that is episodic and controlled by topical rather than strictly chronological or character divisions engenders a novel that some readers might wish were tighter. In such a structure, many of the characters (Stormgren's kidnappers, Rupert Boyce and his wife) are one-dimensional. The two characters in the prologue, Reinhold and Schneider, never appear again. In fact, the first section of the novel, which in most cases is the source of much information about the plot, voice, and structure, is not crucial to the development of the narrative or style. Finally, while the use of the characteristics of the devil for the Overlords is clever, the explanation for this appearance given by Karellen at the end is unconvincing: the Overlords had never come to earth before, but the image of the devil was humanity's "future memory" of its ruinous encounter with the Overlords.

47

Childhood's End may seem to some readers a flawed novel, but it does exhibit *fitness*. It is unified by the continued development of understanding of the Overlords, by the character of Karellen, by a pattern of characterization, and by a pattern of images, some of them religious.

Teaching Suggestions

Since this novel involves beings from another planet, teaching aids will largely be limited to fictional occurrences. A major feature of *Childhood's End* is a modern conception of the devil. A possible student assignment is the tracing of past portraits of the devil, especially those that place him in modern (nonbiblical) times, and comparing these portraits with that in *Childhood's End*. Some examples are Christopher Marlowe's play *The Tragical History of Doctor Faustus*, Stephen Vincent Benet's *The Devil and Daniel Webster* (play and story), and Ira Levin's *Rosemary's Baby*.

A drama suitable for class performance that also posits the invasion of earth by superintelligent beings is Gore Vidal's *Visit to a Small Planet* (in *Visit to a Small Planet and Other Television Plays*, ed. Gore Vidal, Little, Brown, 1957). It exists as a TV drama running around an hour and as a full-length play. Although it was also made into a feature film in 1960 starring Jerry Lewis, the only elements the film has in common with the Vidal original are the title, the basic situation, and four lines of script.

4. Media as Teaching Aids

Drama

Earlier in this report, the theoretical difficulties with science fiction drama were examined. Following the lead of Tolkien's "On Fairy Stories," it was noted that the scientific verisimilitude necessary for science fiction might be difficult to attain with the illusionary atmosphere of the theater. Also, there are relatively few such plays to use in judging whether or not science fiction drama is possible. Below is a list of some attempts at science fiction drama. All of these dramas are open to criticism as legitimate science fiction. Shaw's *Back to Methuselah*, while it has a science fiction premise and has been influential in science fiction history, is only superficially scientific and proves fanciful in its execution, beginning in the Garden of Eden and ending with a dream epilogue. Čapek's *R.U.R.*, in addition to being somewhat stiff as drama by contemporary standards, is caught in the depths of German romanticism. *Warp* has affinities with the comic strip, and *Visit to a Small Planet* ends as an intellectual joke. Even Isaac Asimov's "The Last Question" has to cheat on the scientific explanations. When all energy transfer has stopped, a computer continues trying to find a solution. In order for the computer to function in the absence of energy, Asimov has had to draw a mystical distinction between matter energy and mind energy which can be conserved.

In spite of this, all these dramas are suitable as supportive material for classroom activities. They can stimulate class interest. They can provide visual as well as written examples of treatments of science fiction themes. They are especially helpful in demonstrating human reactions to science fiction situations.

Although there are not many attempts at science fiction drama, there are some additional one-act plays that are suitable for classroom use. Students, should be encouraged to seek examples of this form in performing-arts periodicals and books.

Back to Methuselah by George Bernard Shaw. 1922. *Complete Plays with Prefaces.* Vol. II, Dodd, Mead, and Co., 1963. Also Penguin paperback.

Play cycle composed of five plays. "In the Beginning," Part One, is a retelling of the story of Adam and Eve who learn from the Serpent the secret of the Life Force. Part Two, "The Gospel of the Brothers Barnabas," shows the rediscovery of the secret of prolonging one's life. In Part Three, "The Thing Happens," set in the year 2170, two individuals from Part Two have survived by unconsciously willing it. In Part Four, "The Tragedy of the Elderly Gentleman," the world in 3000 A.D. is divided into longlivers and shortlivers. Part Five, "As Far As Thought Can Reach," is set in 31,920. Life is once again limitless, as it was in the Garden of Eden. Very long and seldom produced, the cycle still demonstrates the wonder and vision typical of science fiction. Parts Three and Five are the most skillfully written for dramatic purposes, and both provide portraits of the future. These parts and other excerpts from the play cycle are suitable for class presentation or reading aloud.

The Last Question by Isaac Asimov. Written 1966. Produced at the Vanderbilt Planetarium, Long Island, New York, Aug.–Sept. 1975.

Entropy, a term coined by the mathematician Clausius about a century ago, is a state in which all matter is at uniform temperature and therefore no energy transfer is possible. The last question, "Can entropy be reversed?" is posed to a computer several times in the course of the play. When entropy is reached, the computer keeps working to answer the last question. The play runs about an hour.

R.U.R. by Joseph and Karel Capek. 1921. Often anthologized.

A scientist who tries to make robots more humanoid causes them to revolt and destroy humankind. In the end the robots have become very human after all.

Visit to a Small Planet by Gore Vidal. TV drama 1955 (*Visit to a Small Planet and Other TV Plays*, Gore Vidal, ed. Little, Brown, 1957, pap.), Broadway production 1957. The TV version is more readily available and probably more suitable for class use since it runs about an hour. The play version is overextended for the relatively simple premise.

The earth is taken over by a telepathic and seemingly all-powerful visitor from another planet who comes dressed in a Civil War uniform, having overshot the time in which he wanted to arrive. He is about to drive the earth into a third world war when he is reclaimed by another interplanetary visitor and labeled an infant who has escaped from his nursery.

Warp by Stuart Gordon and Bury St. Edmund. A trilogy. First presented at the Organic Theatre in Chicago. Broadway performance at Ambassador Theater. 1973 performance in Washington, D.C. Not yet published.

This Buck-Rogersish excursion is divided into three parts which can be performed as a whole or separately: "My Butterfly, My Body"; "Slither Lust"; and "To Die . . . Alive."

Films

Science fiction films are an object of study in themselves. (See Ralph Amelio, *Hal in the Classroom: Science Fiction Films*, Cincinnati, Ohio: Pflaum/Standard, 1974.) Studying film scripts as literature is difficult because a script is only a blueprint for the final visual, as well as audio, effect of a film. Science fiction films do, however, have an advantage over drama in that special effects, in theory at least, help achieve scientific verisimilitude. And science fiction feature films can be used in a literature classroom either because they are adaptations of specific works or because they are original film scripts that illustrate the outlook and methodology of science fiction.

The Time Machine (1960) is a good example of a film adaptation of a science fiction novel suitable for a literature class. While the film simplifies the Wellsian ideology and the plot, with the aid of George Pal's special effects it provides visual descriptions of the future that even surpass the effects achieved in Wells' prose. A device used in the film to illustrate the Time Traveler's advancing through time is a store mannequin across the street. As the Time Traveler presses the lever gently, the mannequin's clothes are changed in seconds by fast-moving store employees. As the Time Traveler continues pressing the lever forward, the mannequin models in quick succession the clothes styles of two generations—an instant fashion show of popular tastes.

An example of an original screenplay is *Things To Come* (1936) by H. G. Wells. With a time span of over one hundred years, the film traces the future history of the world from world war (the film is alarmingly exact in its prophecy of World War II) to a return to feudalism to utopian society to space flight. A film of imaginative design and at times poetic writing, the film is the epitome of science fiction film making. It is appropriate for a literature class in science fiction, especially a class in which Wells' writing is studied.

Reference has already been made in this report to the use of some films in teaching science fiction as literature. Below is an annotated list of film adaptations of science fiction works. Distributors' names and addresses have been provided whenever available.

The teacher should be aware of two built-in problems with showing feature films in a literature classroom. One, the films are not intended to be treated as content for a course in film study but rather as supportive material for a literature course. Two, teachers and students both should keep in mind that film adaptation of science fiction works or any literature for that matter are just that—adaptations. Some films merely streamline the originals, utilizing advantages that film has over prose. Some films completely change the original, as does Byron Haskin's adaptation of Wells' *The War of the Worlds* which updates the novel to modern day Southern California and takes from the Wells' original the title, the premise, and the film's beginning and end. The teacher must decide if a film adaptation radically different from the original is useful or detrimental to his or her teaching a specific work. Often literature classes can compare general differences between the film and the written work. For example, in the film version of Pierre Boulle's *The Planet of the Apes*, the scenarists, Rod Serling and Michael Wilson, omitted many of the hero's experiences as detailed in the novel, emphasized action sequences such as the hunt thereby giving the film pace, and transposed the hero's realization that the ape planet is earth in the future—a minor climax in the book—to the end of the film where it becomes the major climax. However, such changes, and the emphasis on action in the film dilute the Swiftian satire that seemed to be the novel's main purpose. In film adaptations of literature, some things seem improved, but other things may be lost in the process.

List of Film Adaptations of Science Fiction Works

Andromeda Strain. 1971. Director: Robert Wise. Based on Michael Crichton's book. Cast: Arthur Hill, David Wayne, Kate Reid. Available from Universal 16, 221 Park Avenue, S. New York, New York 10003. 131 min.

A deadly bacteria is brought back to earth from space. A team of research scientists work in an underground lab to try to identify the bacteria and defeat it. The film attempts to recapture the clinical scientific detail of the original with a low-key realistic approach. Without the narrative of the novel, the plot is rather simple and uninteresting and the approach to the film makes the whole thing very dull though the film is well enough produced.

The Day of the Triffids. Great Britain. 1963. D: Steve Schely. Screenplay: Philip Yordan, based on the novel by John Wyndham. Cast: Howard Keel, Nicole Maurey, Janet Scott, Kieron Moore. Available from Hurlock-Cine-World, 13 Arcadia Rd., Old Greenwich, Ct. 06870. 94 min.

A shower of meteors blinds its viewers and mutates extraterrestial plants into carnivorous giants. Studio sets with emphasis on shock effects, but a faithful adaptation of Wyndham novel.

The Day the Earth Stood Still. 1951. D: Robert Wise. Sc: Edmund H. North, b/o "Farewell to the Master" by Harry Bates. Cast: Michael Rennie, Patricia Neal, Hugh Marlowe, Sam Jaffe. Available from Films Incorporated, 4420 Oakton St., Stokie, Ill. 60076. 92 min.

Human-like figure and robot arrive in flying saucer and exhibit great powers. The humanoid is killed but brought back to life by the robot. Adaptation of Bates' story changes plot line (in original the robot turned out to be the master), emphasizes Christ-parallel and world peace message. Very good production. One of the best of the 1950's science fiction films.

Fahrenheit 451. Great Britain/France. 1966. D: François Truffaut. Sc: François Truffaut, Jean Louis Richard, b/o novel by Ray Bradbury. Available from Swank Motion Pictures, 201 S. Jefferson Ave., St. Louis, Mo. 63166. 112 min. Cast: Oscar Werner, Julie Christie, Cyril Cusak, Anton Diffring.

Faithful, well produced version of Bradbury's novel, but very slow, harmed by casting Julie Christie in double role of hero's wife and mistress.

First Men on the Moon. Great Britain. 1964. D: Nathan Juran. Sc: Nigel Kneale, Jan Reed, b/o novel by H. G. Wells. Cast: Edward Judd, Martha Hyer, Lionel Jeffries.

Adapted with the help of science fiction scenarist Kneale, this version of the Wells' novel tacks on a modern prologue and epilogue of the astronauts finding an ancient British flag on the moon, then goes into a flashback of the flight of three Victorians there. Captures Wells' irony and humor. Excellent.

The Incredible Shrinking Man. 1957. D: Jack Arnold. Sc: Richard Matheson, from his novel. Cast: Grant Williams, Randy Stuart, April Kent. 81 min.

Matheson's adaptation of his own novel is workmanlike, but on the whole it is a rather simplistic and didactic trick film of a man who breathes a mysterious vapor and shrinks to a few inches high. Filled with the usual shock effects for such a film: man is chased by a cat, kills a spider, etc.

The Invisible Man. 1933. D: James Whale. Sc: R. C. Sherriff, Philip Wylie, b/o novel by H. G. Wells. Cast: Claude Rains, Gloria Stuart, William Harrigan, Henry Travers. 74 min.

The British village atmosphere has been retained from the original and the special effects convincingly represent invisibility in this fine film adaptation of the Wells' novel. Humorous, exciting, well played.

Nineteen Eighty Four. Great Britain. 1956. D: Michael Anderson. Sc: William P. Templeton, Ralph Bettinson, b/o novel by George Orwell. Cast: Edmond O'Brien, Jan Sterling, Michael Redgrave. Available from Macmillan Audio Brandon, 8400 Brookfield Ave., Brookfield, Ill., 60513. 91 min.

Two endings were filmed (one happy, one sad), which says a good deal about this adaptation of the Orwell novel about a future police state and one man's attempt to rise above it. Two American stars are miscast and the whole thing becomes rather romanticized.

The Omega Man. 1971. D: Boris Sagel, b/o novel *I Am A Legend* by Richard Matheson. Cast: Charlton Heston. 98 min.

Second film version of Matheson novel (the first was the 1964 Italian-made *Last Man on Earth* with Vincent Price) of the last person on earth who is constantly attacked by vampires in an otherwise empty world. Good production though it suffers from the plot having become standard fare and from interpolated social commentary.

Planet of the Apes. 1967. D: Franklin J. Schaffner. Sc: Rod Serling, Michael Wilson, b/o novel by Pierre Boulle. Cast: Charlton Heston, Roddy McDowall, Kim Hunter, Maurice Evans, James Whitmore, James Daly. Available from Films Incorporated. 112 min.

Astronauts go into the future and land on a planet ruled by apes. The adapters have given the original story pace, a climax, and dramatic ending, but have abandoned the Swiftian satire which was the novel's whole point and put in its place supposedly satiric lines such as "People see, people do." Fantastic production, well cast and popular enough to occasion four sequels and a television series and perhaps revive interest in the science fiction film. A word of warning: the four sequels get further and further away from the original novel and actually become quite confusing if you try to follow them in sequence.

The Thing. 1951. D: Christian Nyby. Sc: Charles Lederer, b/o story "Who Goes There" by John Campbell Jr. Cast: Kenneth Tobey, Margaret Sheridan, Robert Cornwaithe, James Arness. Available from Films Incorporated. 87 min.

An alien being threatens a research team at the North Pole. This story is a good example of how science fiction is adapted for films. In the original, the alien was an intelligent, chameleon type creature. In the film, he is an irrational Frankenstein-type monster. An exciting film in itself but a poor version of the story.

The Time Machine. 1960. D: George Pal. Sc: David Duncan, b/o novel by H. G. Wells. Cast: Rod Taylor, Yvette Mimieux, Alan Young, Sebastian Cabot. Available from Films Incorporated. 103 min.

A man invents a time machine and travels into the future to view a world where intelligence and luxury have made humans weak and prey for the carnivorous Morlocks. The film omits the future trips made by the Time Traveler and the death of the girl and is, therefore, more optimistic about the future than the book really is. Sumptuously produced, well paced, the special effects reproduce time travel almost better than Wells describes it.

Village of the Damned. Great Britain. 1960. D: Wolf Rilla. Sc: Sterling Silliphant, Wolf Rilla, George Barclay, b/o novel *The Midwich Cuckoos* by John Wyndham. Cast: George Sanders, Barbara Shelley, Michael Gwenn, Laurence Naismith. Available from Films Incorporated. 78 min.

A small English town is lulled to sleep by aliens and all child-bearing women impregnated. The resulting children are blonde-haired, strange, and intellectual giants. A quiet, unnerving film adaptation of the Wyndham novel, a little slow but well produced, well acted by a good cast (especially Sanders).

The War of the Worlds. 1953. D: Bryon Haskin. Sc: Barre Lyndon, b/o novel by H. G. Wells. Cast: Gene Barry, Ann Robinson, Henry Brandon. Available from Films Incorporated. 85 min.

Though some have found it exciting, this version of the Wells' novel is a travesty of the original. A plot updating to modern Southern California allows the Martians to weather the effects of an atomic blast. The film loses the claustrophobic effect of the original English-based novel. A romantic subplot has been developed. A much better Wells' adaptation is *First Men on the Moon*, referenced earlier, which does not update the plot but provides a modern framework.

When Worlds Collide. 1951. D: Rudolph Mate. Sc: Sydney Boehm, b/o novel by Edwin Balmer, Philip Wylie. Cast: Richard Derr, Barbara Rush, John Hoyt, Larry Keating. Available from Films Incorporated. 82 min.

Two heavenly bodies are about to collide with earth, so preparation races ahead on a rocket ship that will take selected individuals from the earth to safety in outer space. Faithful to the original, good special effects, but dated in the dramatics, slow, and a little boring.

Television and Radio

Science fiction as adapted or created for television is a handy teaching tool because of the accessibility of television to students. A teacher may find it frustrating, however, to have to adapt a curriculum schedule to that of television stations, especially when they are showing reruns of a series. It is a good idea for teachers to keep abreast of local and network programming, in order to suggest appropriate class viewing. Some television series such as *Star Trek* or *Lost in Space* are within the science fiction domain and are frequently re-run by local stations. The *Twilight Zone, Outer Limits,* and *Night Gallery* series, presently in syndication, are anthology series dealing with general speculative themes and featuring original science fiction scripts of interest as well as adaptations of science fiction works. Frederick Brown's "Arena," for example, was adapted for both the *Outer Limits* and *Star Trek.* Mary Shelley's "The Mortal Immortal" was seen in uncredited adaptation on both the *Twilight Zone* and *Star Trek.*

Television, however, often experiences problems with a major requirement of science fiction: scientific verisimilitude in the illusionary world of make-believe. Science fiction film is at least able to utilize special effects to offset some of this difficulty. Because of the viewing time factor involved television special effects seldom equal those of the movies. Also, television series have the added problem of the nature of the television system: things that do not work are often changed without explanation; new ideas are added; different writers from episode to episode mar the consistency of approach; a story must be either padded or crammed with detail in order to fit into a twenty-four or fifty minute setup; continuing characters are dropped when a salary dispute or another acting commitment occurs; and radical changes are effected in the second or third season to buoy up the ratings. For example, in *Star Trek,* which was an earnest attempt at a television science fiction series, in the course of the first season Mr. Spock's ears were shortened; his "nerve pinch," unknown in the early episodes, was invented; and, as authors varied from script to script, Vulcan powers Mr. Spock was able to employ in one episode were somehow lacking to him in another. In the third year of the series, a slicker and more contemporary approach was tried; at the end of the third year the series was cancelled.

Whatever its deficiencies, television science fiction, when available, is good supportive material for a literature class in science fiction. Programs offer a good starting point for short critical essays, as well as discussions comparing written and dramatized forms.

Television toyed with science fiction early in its history with *Captain Video* and *Superman*. The British did interesting things with Nigel Kneale's Quartermas specials, all of which were later made into feature films. But these are generally not available on television today. Below is an annotated list of television series which might reappear on local channels, which more or less fall within the science fiction domain.

Lost In Space. This CBS show lasted several seasons as a space version of *Swiss Family Robinson.* Obvious studio sets. Some interesting episodes but often indulges in pure fantasy. Usually geared toward the younger children.

Kolchak: The Night Stalker. This ABC show, which lasted one season, was derived from two highly successful TV movies. The first, *The Night Stalker*, follows the reporter Kolchak's investigation of the appearance of a vampire in modern day Chicago. The second, *The Night Strangler*, finds Kolchak pursuing a ghoul that prowls modern day Seattle. The series suffers from trying to duplicate the success of the movies as Kolchak encounters vampires, Jack the Ripper, and some scientifically based monsters all in modern locations. Some individual episodes are very good.

The Invaders. This series lasted several seasons. One man knows of the existence of invaders from another planet who, in human form, are trying to take over the earth. The series shows his attempts to convince people of the invaders' existence.

Night Gallery. This NBC anthology series ran several seasons. Two or three playlets filled both an hour and a half hour format. Inclined to pure fantasy, though some episodes are futuristically and scientifically based. Created by Rod Serling.

The Outer Limits. This series lasted one and a half seasons. An anthology that proved often startling in its conceptions. One episode, "The Shape of Things Unknown" is especially noteworthy. Two women murder their lover only to have the murdered man brought back to life by the strange young Mr. Hobart. Sir Cedric Hardwicke plays a butler who intones, "My Mr. Hobart tinkers with time. Just as time has tinkered with Mr. Hobart."

Star Trek. This series ran three seasons on NBC. It was brought back by popular demand after having been cancelled in the second season. Good production values, some scripts written by known science fiction writers, though the series suffers from the repetition of one device: the star ship visits worlds somehow modeled after episodes from earth history—1920 Chicago, ancient Rome, Tombstone, Nazi Germany. To placate angry viewers who objected to the series' cancellation, a cartoon series was initiated using many of the original cast. The cartoon series is rather fancifully conceived, however.

The Time Tunnel. An ABC series that lasted one season. Describes the adventures of two scientists lost in a time tunnel. Every episode takes them to a famous historical event.

The Twilight Zone. This famous, often syndicated Rod Serling series is more pure fantasy than science fiction. However, some of the episodes in this anthology deal with science fiction topics: the last people on earth theme was used several times.

Voyage to the Bottom of the Sea. This CBS series lasted four seasons. It began as a spy show, dabbled in science fiction, and finally ended in kiddie-oriented space fantasy. One or two episodes of interest.

References

Chapter One—What Is Science Fiction?

1. Damon Knight, *One Hundred Years of Science Fiction* (New York: Simon and Schuster, 1968), p.8.
2. Kingsley Amis, *New Maps of Hell: A Survey of Science Fiction* (New York: Harcourt, Brace and Company, 1960), p.18.
3. Sam Moskowitz, *Explorers of the Infinite: Shapers of Science Fiction* (New York: World Books, 1957), p.11.
4. Donald Wollheim, *The Universe Makers* (New York: Harper & Row, 1971), p.10.
5. "Classification," *Dictionary of World Literature*, James Shipley, ed. (Totowa, New Jersey: Littlefield, Adams and Co., 1968), p.62.
6. For further discussion of the generic literary classification of science fiction, consult "On the Poetics of the Science Fiction Genre," by Darko Suvin in *College English*, December 1972, pp. 372–82. Suvin writes as follows: "SF is, then, a literary genre whose necessary and sufficient conditions are the presence and interaction of estrangement and cognition, and whose main formal device is an imaginative framework alternative to the author's empirical framework." (p.375)
7. Lin Carter, *Imaginary Worlds* (New York: Ballantine, 1973), p.6.
8. J. R. R. Tolkien, "On Fairy Stories," *Essays Presented to Charles Williams* (1947, rpt. Grand Rapids: Wm. B. Eerdmans, 1966), p.67.
9. Amis, p.23.
10. Tolkien, p.69.
11. John Aquino, "Shaw and C. S. Lewis' Space Trilogy," *Shaw Review*, pp.28–32, Jan. 1975.
12. Daniel J. Leary, "The Ends of Childhood: Eschatology in Shaw and Clarke," *Shaw Review*, pp.67–78, May 1973.
13. J. R. Christopher, "Methuselah Out of Heinlein by Shaw," *Shaw Review*, pp. 79–88, May 1973.

Chapter Two—Science Fiction in the Classroom

1. *Publisher's Weekly*, Nov. 11, 1974, p.58.
2. Barbara Gay Ford and Ronald D. Ford, "Science Fiction: Curriculum for the Future," *Learning*, pp.32–3, May/June 1975.
3. Dave Samuelson, "Proposal for the Mandatory Use of Science Fiction in the General Curriculum." Paper presented at the Annual Meeting of the National Council of Teachers of English, November 1971. ERIC Document ED 089 277.
4. Joseph D. Olander, Martin H. Greenberg, Patricia Warrick, *School and Society Through Science Fiction* (Chicago: Rand McNally, 1975).
5. P. Sandberg, "Science Fiction and Legitimate Science," *South Australian Science Teachers Journal*, pp. 35–6, April 1973.
6. Beverly Friend, "Strange Bedfellows: Science Fiction, Linguistics and Education," *English Journal*, pp.998–1003, October 1973.

7. H. L. Drake, "General Semantics and Science Fiction in the Speech Communication Classroom." Paper presented at the Annual Meeting of the Speech Communication Association, November 1973. ERIC Document ED 084 580.
8. *Social Education,* February 1973. (Theme Issue: World History Through Science Fiction)
9. Alan W. Wohfeil, "Science Fiction Stories in the Social Studies Classroom," *Clearinghouse,* pp.300–304, January 1970.
10. Bernard C. Hollister, Deane C. Thompson, *Grokking the Future: Science Fiction in the Classroom* (Dayton: Pflaum/Standard, 1973).
11. Dave Samuelson, p.8.
12. Shelia Schwartz, "Science Fiction as Humanistic Study," 1971. ERIC Document ED 061 201.
13. Alvin Toffler, *Future Shock* (New York: Bantam, 1970), p.425.
14. For a detailed history and analysis of this stage of the development of science fiction, consult James Gunn, "Science Fiction and the Mainstream," *Science Fiction, Today and Tomorrow* (Baltimore: Penguin, 1974), pp.183–214.
15. James Blish, "The Tale That Wags the Gods," *American Libraries,* December 1970, p.1031.
16. Theodore Sturgeon, "Science Fiction, Morals, and Religion," *Science Fiction, Today and Tomorrow,* Reginald Bretnor, ed. (Baltimore: Penguin, 1974), p.98.
17. Alexei Oanshin, "Science Fiction Bibliography and Criticism," *American Libraries,* October 1970, pp.884–5.
18. Robert Scholes, *Structural Fabulation: An Essay of Fiction of the Future* (University of Notre Dame Press, 1975), p.18.
19. *Ibid.,* p.23.
20. Northrop Frye, *Anatomy of Criticism* (1957; rpt. Princeton: Princeton University Press, 1971), p.49.
21. Robert Silverberg, "After the Myths Went Home," *Tomorrow, and Tomorrow, and Tomorrow* (New York: Holt, Rinehart and Winston, 1975), p.269.
22. Olaf Stapledon, *Last and First Men* (1930; rpt. Baltimore: Penguin, 1972), pp.11–12.
23. Blish, p.1033.
24. George Bernard Shaw, *Back to Methuselah, Complete Plays with Prefaces,* Vol. II (New York: Dodd, Mead & Co., 1963), p.617.
25. H. G. Wells, *Things To Come* (New York: Macmillan, 1935), pp.154–5.

Chapter Three—Methods of Teaching Science Fiction as Literature

1. Frederick Brown, "Arena," *Tomorrow, and Tomorrow, and Tomorrow,* ed. Frank Herbert and others (New York: Holt, Rinehart and Winston, 1974), pp.276–7.
2. H. P. Lovecraft, "The Shadow Out of Time," *The Colour Out of Space* (New York: Lancer Books, 1963), p.156.
3. John Wyndham, *The Midwich Cuckoos* (New York: Ballantine Books, 1957), p.3.

4. Robert Heinlein, "The Year of the Jackpot," *Looking Ahead: A Vision of Science Fiction*, ed. Dick Allen (New York: Harcourt Brace and Jovanovich, Inc., 1975), p.294.

5. Mary S. Weinkauf, "Breaking the Discipline Barriers: Practical Uses of Science Fiction," *Delta Kappa Gamma Bulletin*, Spring, 1975, p.33.

6. Darko Suvin, "On the Poetics of the Science Fiction Genre," *College English*, December 1972, p.374.

7. Ray Bradbury, *The Martian Chronicles* (New York: Bantam, 1970), p.14.

8. Donald Wollheim, *The Universe Makers* (New York: Harper and Row, 1971), p.6.

9. C. S. Lewis, "On Science Fiction," *Of Other Worlds: Essays and Stories* (New York: Harcourt, Brace and World, 1966).

10. Suzanne Millies, *Science Fiction Primer for Teachers* (Dayton, Ohio: Pflaum/Standard, 1975).

11. Wollheim, p.16.

Bibliography

Amis, Kingsley. *New Maps of Hell: A Survey of Science Fiction.* New York: Harcourt, Brace, and Co., 1960.

Bretnor, Reginald, ed. *Science Fiction, Today and Tomorrow.* Baltimore: Penguin, 1974.

Hollister, Bernard C.; Thompson, Deane C. *Grokking the Future: Science Fiction in the Classroom.* Dayton: Pflaum/Standard, 1973.

Knight, Damon. *In Search of Wonder.* 2nd edition. Chicago: Advent, 1967.

Lewis, C. S. *Of Other Worlds.* New York: Harcourt, Brace, and World, 1966.

Moskowitz, Sam. *Explorers of the Infinite: Shapes of Science Fiction.* New York: World Books, 1957.

Samuelson, Dave. "Proposal for the Mandatory Use of Science Fiction in the General Curriculum." Paper presented at the Annual Meeting of the National Council of Teachers of English, November 1971. ERIC Document, ED 089 277.

Scholes, Robert. *Structural Fabulation: An Essay on Fiction of the Future.* Notre Dame, Indiana: University of Notre Dame Press, 1975.

Suvin, Darko. "On the Poetics of the Science Fiction Genre," *College English* (December 1973), 372–382.

Wollheim, Donald A. *The Universe Makers.* New York: Harper and Row, 1971.

These Acknowledgments are continued from page 4:

From "The Day of the Jackpot" by Robert Heinlein. Copyright © 1952, Galaxy Publishing Co. Reprinted by permission of Lurton Blassingame, the author's agent.

From "Her strong enchantments failing" by A. E. Housman. From THE COLLECTED POEMS OF A. E. HOUSMAN. Copyright 1922 by Holt, Rinehart and Winston. Copyright 1950 by Barclays Bank Ltd. Reprinted by permission of Holt, Rinehart and Winston, Publishers. By permission also of The Society of Authors as the literary representatives of the Estate of A. E. Housman; and Jonathan Cape Ltd., publishers of A. E. Housman's COLLECTED POEMS.

From "The Shadow Out of Time" by H. P. Lovecraft. Reprinted by permission of Arkham House Publishers, Inc., Sauk City, Wisconsin.

From "After the Myths Went Home" by Robert Silverberg. By permission of the author's agents, Scott Meredith Literary Agency Inc., 845 Third Ave., New York, New York 10022.

From LAST AND FIRST MEN by Olaf Stapledon. © 1930 by Olaf Stapledon. By permission of Penguin Books.

From FUTURE SHOCK by Alvin Toffler. Copyright © 1970. Reprinted by Random House, Inc.

From "On Fairy Stories" by J. R. R. Tolkien. By permission of the Houghton Mifflin Company.

From THINGS TO COME by H. G. Wells. By permission of The Estate of H. G. Wells.

From "The Star" by H. G. Wells. Reprinted by permission of Collins-Knowlton-Wing and the Estate of the late H. G. Wells. Copyright © 1952 by Dover Publications, copyright © 1905 by Charles Scribner & Son, copyright © 1932 by H. G. Wells.